Contents

KU-040-171

Plumbing
Floors and Flooring
Insulation

Walter Gundrey

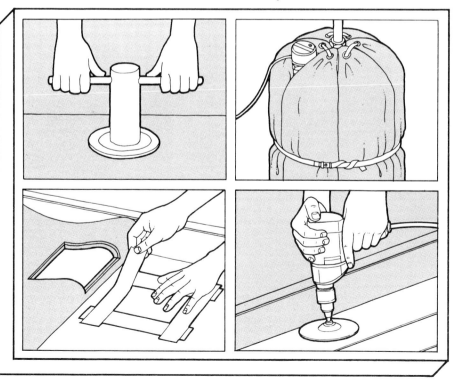

WARD LOCK LIMITED · LONDON

© Text Elizabeth Gundrey and Walter Gundrey 1985

© Illustrations Ward Lock Limited 1985

First published in Great Britain in 1985
by Ward Lock Limited, 82 Gower Street,
London WC1E 6EQ.

Text set in Plantin Light
by MS Filmsetting Limited, Frome, Somerset

Printed and bound in Finland

British Library Cataloguing in Publication Data

Gundrey, Elizabeth
    Home repairs; plumbing, floor and flooring,
    insulation.
    1. Dwellings – Maintenance and repair –
    Amateurs' manuals
    I. Title
    643'.7   TH4827.3

    ISBN 0-7063-6368-X

Introduction

For those of little skill

To call a tradesman to one's home these days costs several pounds, no matter how trifling the job that has to be done. This is particularly hard on people of limited means – and it is often quite unnecessary.

This book is about jobs that can be undertaken by a complete amateur. They call for no previous experience or skill, and need a minimum of very ordinary tools. The book is written in everyday language, avoiding technical jargon wherever possible.

The main essential is to have the right tools – few of them but well chosen (see the beginning of each section).

Tenants and leaseholders

Unless you own the freehold of your house, some repairs may be the landlord's responsibility rather than yours. This is particularly likely to be the case in flats where certain services are common to more than one home. Examples are drains, the cold water supply, and gutters and downpipes. It is normally up to the landlord to repair 'common parts', such as staircases or paths, in a shared building, and to see to things like the roof which are part of the main structure of any rented property. If the landlord fails to keep these repaired, any Citizens' Advice Bureau or Legal Advice Centre will tell you what to do. Be careful about undertaking any repairs to such things yourself: in particular, you would be liable for any damage you might do.

Fixtures within your home are also the landlord's property, but an obligation to keep them in good order is normally the tenant's: examples are baths, basins, sinks, WCs, and taps. If you go further and put in improvements, these become the landlord's property: examples are new doorbells or WC seats – unless you were to replace the old ones when you move out.

Your insurance policy

You (or your landlord) should have a policy covering the building, and you should also have one that covers its contents. One policy may combine both. Your building policy will be in the hands of your building society if your house is mortgaged.

Such policies cover fire, flood, theft and some other disasters too. You may be able to claim for the cost of putting right the following mishaps – whether you do them yourself or not. Outbuildings, gates and so forth are likely to be covered too. But don't expect a claim to succeed if the cause of the damage is really old age or neglect; and claim immediately the damage occurs, starting on the repair only if it is so urgent that it cannot await the insurance company's reaction.

Flooding from cracked tank or pipes. (Damage to carpets, or even dry rot, may qualify for a claim, but not replacement of the tank or pipes. Keep the damaged goods as the insurance company may want to inspect them.)

Flooding from cracked basin, WC, etc. (The replacement of these will probably be covered, but not if you caused the crack while carrying out repairs.)

Flooding from blocked drain, rusted gutters, etc. (Less likely to qualify because blockages are usually due to negligence).

Damage to underground pipes is covered in some policies.

If a tenant, you are also likely to have rights under your landlord's insurance policy for the structure as a whole: see above.

Many policies require the policyholder to foot the bill for the first £15 or so of certain types of repair.

Repairs and your mortgage

When you get a mortgage loan you may have part of it withheld until (for example) dry rot or a defective damp-proof course are put right. Find out whether your building society will or won't accept do-it-yourself repairs before embarking on such things.

The society will require you to keep the house in good repair. It will also require you to ask permission before making any major alteration, such as changing from one type of window to another (you may find you need permission from the local council too).

If you have it in mind to improve the house in some way, an extra loan may be available to cover the cost.

Repairs and grants

Local councils do not ordinarily give grants for repairs or decorations – except, sometimes, when these are inseparable from grant-aided improvements such as putting in a bath, WC, etc., or if they bring an old house up to modern standards (putting in a damp-proof course, for example). Grants are also available towards the cost of home insulation. Some councils are more flexible than others, but there are always many strings attached to grants and usually weeks or months of delay before you may start work. Full details are in leaflets obtainable from your local council.

When you cannot do it yourself

There is nothing to beat personal recommendation when it comes to choosing a builder or other craftsman. Failing that, membership of a trade association is often some guarantee of reliability. Avoid the type of man who turns up unannounced at the front door with some 'bargain' offer.

Unless a craftsman belongs to a firm, it is best to phone outside working hours. Get an estimate for any small job before he starts: this is not so binding as a written quotation, but is a good deterrent to overcharging

6

later. For big jobs, get written estimates from several – one might quote twice as much as another, but might be providing a more elaborate or better quality job, so read and compare descriptions carefully. Those who advertise an emergency service are apt to be expensive.

If you have a complaint that cannot be resolved, take it to the consumer protection department of your local council or to one of the trade associations named below if a member of theirs is involved.

In an emergency, the water authority or even the police may give you names of plumbers. Some water authorities will not only turn off the supply but even change tap washers or ball-valves (free or at a moderate charge).

Hiring gear – big or small

To find a firm that will hire you anything from a screwdriver upwards, look in the yellow pages of the telephone directory under 'hire', 'contractors' or 'plant' or in the National Plant Hire Guide which many libraries have. The Hire Association, 12 Voluntary Place, Wansted, Essex, can supply addresses. Terms vary enormously. Not all firms give instructions for using complex equipment, and it's wise to check the condition it's in and the length of flex if it's electric.

More advice

Here are some addresses that may come in useful when you want major work done:

Glass Federation (6 Mount Row, London W1) will investigate complaints against member firms who do double glazing, etc.

National Cavity Insulation Association (Bremar House, Sale Place, London W2) vets member-firms' wall insulation work and will see that complaints are settled.

Manufacturers are usually very ready to advise on problems and often have good free booklets. Monthly magazines like *Do It Yourself*, *Practical Householder* and *Homemaker* not only have helpful articles but run enquiry departments. *Handyman Which?* publishes comparative test reports on tools and materials. It is available to subscribers to *Which?* (Consumers' Association, 14 Buckingham Street, London WC2).

In addition, there are trade associations through which you can obtain advice on the choice and correct use of materials; or try your nearest Building Centre. The London one is at 26 Store Street, London WC1E 7BT. A visit is more likely to get results than a written enquiry.

Many big cities have such centres, where you can see displays of fittings, materials and equipment, and obtain sheaves of brochures. Those in London, Cambridge, Bristol and Manchester have very good bookshops that sell do-it-yourself books.

The Department of the Environment and the Building Research Establishment both publish numerous leaflets on specific subjects obtainable (for a charge) from HMSO, 49 High Holborn, London WC1V 6HB.

Metrication
Length
Wood and boards are now measured in metres (m) and millimetres (mm). 1mm is one-thousandth of a metre; 1cm (centimetre) is one-hundredth of a metre.

Standard lengths of softwood boards go from 1.8m up to 6.3m (that is, 1m 800mm; 6m 300mm).
Standard widths are 75–150mm.
Standard thicknesses are 16–38mm.

Standard sizes for posts, rails, etc. are 25 × 25 or 38 or 50mm.

Tool sizes are mostly metric now and so are nail sizes, but so far screws are still being measured in inches.

Glass and tiles are measured in mm.
   1mm = about $\frac{1}{25}$in.
   1cm = about $\frac{2}{5}$in.
   1m = about 3ft 3in.

A steel rule or steel tape with both millimetres and inches on it is a necessity now.

1
Plumbing

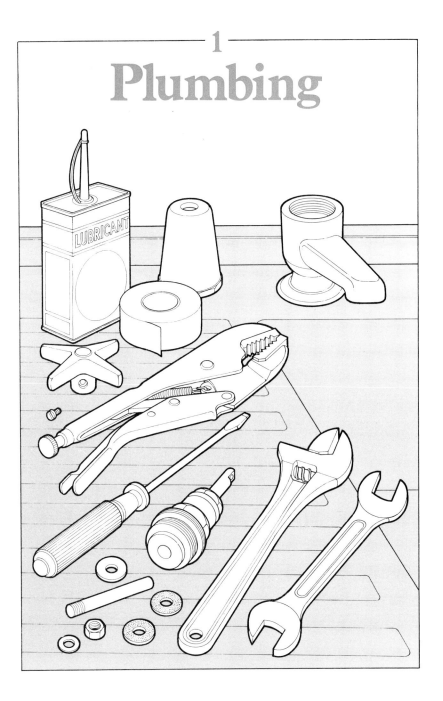

Typical water supply system

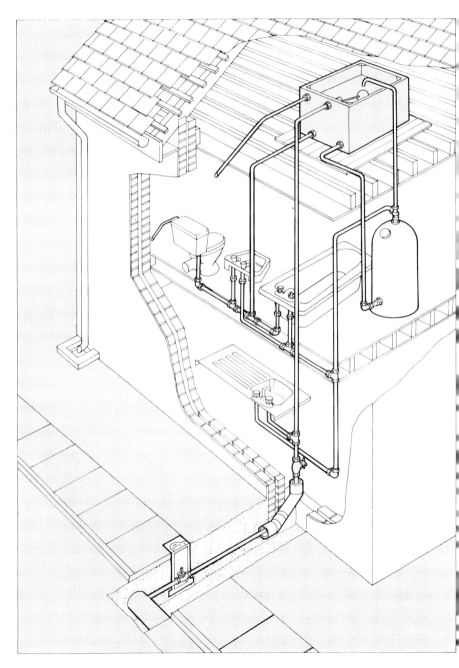

The cold water supply

Whose responsibility?

The water authority is liable only for the public supply running beneath the road and its responsibility ends at the stopcock through which the water enters your service pipe under the ground. This stopcock, usually in a small pit below the pavement but possibly in your garden or cellar, may need a special water authority key to turn it off and on. The water authority is also responsible for sewers, although the actual work involved in looking after them may be done by the local council.

The main service pipe

Normally this gives no trouble unless gardening operations have left it with much less than a metre of soil above, in which case frost may crack it. It ordinarily enters the house via the kitchen floor (at this stage it is usually referred to as the rising main). If it is not embedded in a solid floor but is exposed to the cold air beneath floorboards, it should have been insulated against frost when it was installed.

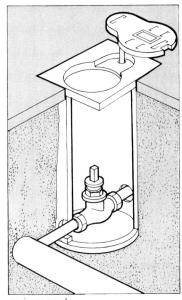

main stopcock

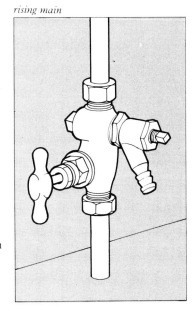

rising main

Turning off the main supply

You should be able to see the rising main under the kitchen sink or elsewhere and, just above floor level, there is usually a stopcock on it which can be turned by hand if the entire water supply needs to be cut off: for instance, if a pipe or tank leaks; while carrying out certain repairs; or when leaving the house vacant for a long period (insurance policies can be invalidated by failing to do this). Above the stopcock may be a drain-cock, operated by a spanner, the purpose of which is to empty the rising main, an operation rarely needed. It has a ridged nozzle so that a hosepipe can be attached.

If you drain off the water supply, also turn off or rake out the boiler or water heaters before these run dry. When turning the water on again, be sure to turn it full

The cold water supply

on – otherwise water pressure will be reduced, with an adverse effect on a shower, automatic washing-machine, the filling of the WC, etc. Because stopcocks can become immovable through prolonged disuse, it is a good idea to turn them off and on again occasionally and to grease the stem. (For methods of releasing stiff ones, see page 13.)

To empty the water system it is, of course, necessary not only to cut off the incoming supply but also to turn taps on and flush the WC, in order to drain the indoor pipes.

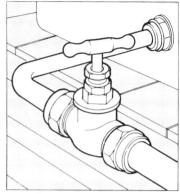

stopcock on pipe from cold tank

Indirect supply

Although in some homes all cold taps and WCs are supplied straight from the rising main, today most water authorities allow only a kitchen cold tap and possibly a non-storage type of water heater (such as an Ascot) to be supplied by branch pipes from it, with all the rest of the water carried up to be stored in a cold-water tank (usually in the attic or occasionally on a flat roof, because the higher it is, the better will be the water pressure and the less likely is its noise to be heard in the house). The reason for this indirect method is largely that it cuts down any risk of contamination getting drawn back into the public supply. It also keeps water pressure constant in the house, and ensures a supply for a while even if the mains water is cut off.

From this tank will descend at least one pipe, with branches serving bathroom taps and WC, while a second will serve any storage-type water heater (such as an electrically heated cylinder). A third may serve a shower. These pipes may have their own isolating stopcocks, usually near the tank, so that if you want to drain only the cold supply to the bathroom you can do so.

If these pipes do not have their own stopcocks, you can cut off the supply to the cold tank by either using the main stopcock under the sink or tying up the arm of the floating ball in the tank, which will close its intake pipe.

tying up ball float

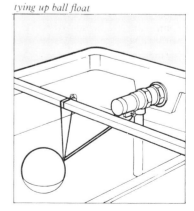

Tools and materials

Undoing connections

The hardest part of plumbing repairs is often getting things undone. With prolonged disuse, screw-threads are apt to seize up, particularly if rust, hard-water scale or paint have worsened matters. Tapping, or pouring boiling water over them, may help. Paint stripper can be used, or a blow-lamp if adjacent surfaces are protected with wet cloths.

Choosing the right tools is essential. Spanners must be exactly the right size for the job, and must grip without slipping. The wrong tools can spoil the shape of nuts, maul and distort pipes, and damage chromium. These pages show the choice available, and which to use for which job.

To help with really stubborn cases, there are dismantling lubricants in cans or aerosols. After applying one of these, give a tightening-up movement to crack any rust or scale before attempting to undo the part. If this does not suffice, give another application and allow it to soak in for a few minutes.

If all else fails, a hacksaw blade may cut through a bolt.

Reassembly

When reassembling things like taps and waste-traps, grease the screw-threads with Vaseline to keep them movable in future.

Where water pipes are concerned, the usual method was to apply a special compound and hemp to the screw-thread before assembling it. This seal does not harden, so that the joint can be unscrewed at a future date if need arises. A newer alternative involving less mess is to wind round the screw-thread a fine tape made of PTFE. This makes an absolute seal but easily comes away if the joint has to be unscrewed later (apply the tape in the same direction as the screw-thread). Plastic joints, though needing no sealing, have screw-threads which tend to jam if not turned carefully: do not force them.

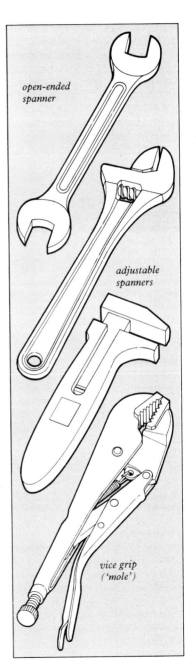

open-ended spanner

adjustable spanners

vice grip ('mole')

Tools and materials

Spanners

Nuts and other components need spanners
to fasten and unfasten them. Because nuts
come in a variety of sizes, some spanners
have adjustable jaws. They are sometimes
referred to as wrenches.

The commonest fixed-jaw spanners are
open-ended. Ring spanners, which exert
more force and can be used in more
confined spaces, are sometimes useful for
plumbing jobs. Some spanners have a ring
at one end and an open end at the other.

Unfortunately, several systems of nut
sizes are in use in Britain, and often they
are not clearly marked. The only way out of
this dilemma is to take the nut to the tool
shop (or motor accessory shop) when you
go to buy a spanner. Do not buy spanners
in large sets containing many sizes you will
never need. You may find it helpful to have
duplicates – one to hold and the other to
turn. Over-long (and over-thick) spanners
can be a nuisance in confined spaces,
although the longer the spanner, the more
force you can exert on it.

Although there are many patent
adjustable spanners, the simple crescent-
jawed or square-jawed type remains the
best for most purposes. A thumb-screw
moves one of the jaws until the right size is
reached – up to 20–30mm, depending
which size you buy.

To hold pipes and other circular things,
you may need a pipe wrench. A Stillson is a
common type, and is made in a range of
sizes. Also useful is a vicegrip, like a pair of
large pliers that can be locked.

Pliers

Pliers have square jaws to grip most things,
a curved portion to hold pipes or nuts, and
a cutting portion with which to sever wires.
(Some have another wire cutter too – a
small groove on the outside.) 175cm (7in)
pliers are popular size, smaller ones will be
more convenient in confined spaces. Thin
jaws are often handier, too. Long-nosed
pliers will often be needed.

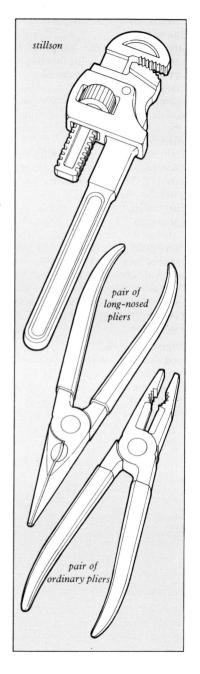

stillson

*pair of
long-nosed
pliers*

*pair of
ordinary pliers*

Tools and materials

Fillers for gaps and cracks
Epoxy putty
Strong, hard, smooth, heatproof. White
(can be painted). Usable for cracks in
pipes, basins, etc. See page 24.
Plastic steel
Epoxy plus steel particles. Very strong,
hard, smooth, heatproof. Fine for metal
pipes.
Silicone rubber
Resilient, strong, smooth. White or
coloured; shiny. Best choice for gaps
around baths and sinks. Can even be
applied under water.
Vinyl adhesive
Specifically for cracks in things like plastic
gutters and rainwater pipes.
Non-setting mastics or sealants
Are usable for joints which may one day
need to be opened up again, but mainly for
filling gaps subject to some movement.
Plastic-based ones are white or grey;
bitumen-based ones, for outdoor use, are
usually black.

Often **waterproof building tapes** are a
good solution to cracks and gaps. Some
have a top surface of aluminium foil. (More
about these on pages 23 and 52, Gutters
and rainwater pipes.)

Some tap types

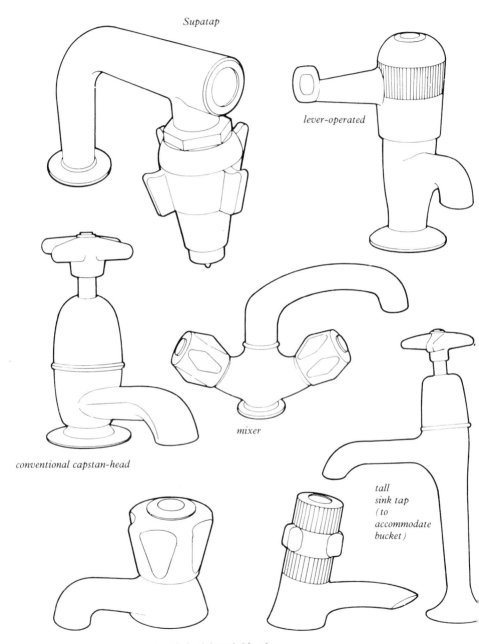

Supatap

lever-operated

conventional capstan-head

mixer

tall
sink tap
(to
accommodate
bucket)

two kinds of shrouded head

Taps – dripping

Note Many water authorities will repair dripping taps without charge

Cause
Washer deteriorated

Tools and materials needed
Washer: 20mm ($\frac{3}{4}$in) for most bath and mixer taps, 15mm ($\frac{1}{2}$in) for most sink and basin taps
Small spanners
Probably large spanner and dismantling lubricant (see page 14)

Method

1 Turn off water supply as follows: for a kitchen cold tap, use main stopcock; for any other, see page 12. You do not need to empty the hot-water cylinder when re-washering a hot tap because the water comes only from the top of the hot cylinder. Turn taps on to drain the pipes.

2 With the tap in the full-on position, remove handle by loosening the screw at the side and then tapping the handle upwards. If it will not move, raise the tap cover and jam a piece of wood or large spanner below, then screw the handle down and lever it off with the wood. Hot water may help to get the tap cover unscrewed by hand. If the tap handle is impossible to shift, it can be left in place if a spanner can be slid beneath the raised tap cover.

3 If a large spanner has to be used to unscrew the tap cover, use sticky-tape or a cloth to protect the metal. Not all tap covers are screwed on clockwise.

4 Having removed the tap cover, use a spanner to undo the large hexagonal nut (hold the body of the tap firmly). Remove the top gear.

5 Pull out the jumper (a brass stem): there may be a split-pin to remove first. Undo its nut. Replace the old washer with a new one of the same size.

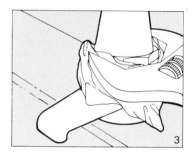

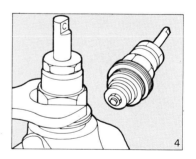

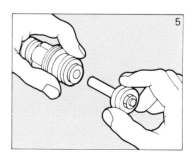

Taps – dripping

6 If even dismantling lubricant will not shift
the nut, a new jumper complete with
washer may have to be bought.
7 When reassembling the tap, grease all
screw-threads (Vaseline or even lard will
do) and do not over-tighten. Take
particular care with plastic ones as it is easy
to jam the screw-thread.
8 If dripping still continues, this means the
valve seating below the jumper needs
replacement. A plastic seating and jumper
unit can be bought, to force down on to the
existing seating. Screw the tap handle hard
down.

Shrouded heads
To remove the combined cover and handle,
prise out the plastic disc on the top to
reveal a screw. When this has been
unscrewed, a firm tug will pull the head off.
Some have no screw but simply pull off;
others have a screw at the side.

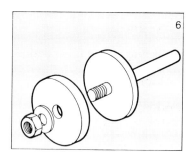

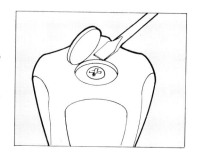

removing a shrouded head

Taps, swivel – dripping

Cause
Washer deteriorated

Tools and materials needed
Long-nosed pliers
Washer(s)

Method
1 There is no need to turn off the water supply. Unscrew or lever up the shroud at the foot of the nozzle.
2 Use the pliers to take out the circular copper clip and slide it up the nozzle.
3 With the nozzle removed, replace the washer (or washers) with new ones. Wet the foot of the nozzle before replacing it.

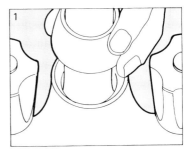

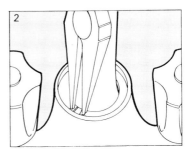

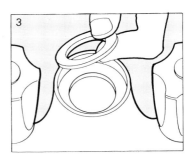

Supataps – dripping

Cause
Washer deteriorated

Tools and materials needed
Spanner
Washer-jumper

Method
1 There is no need to turn off the water supply. Partly open the nozzle and unscrew the nut with the spanner. Detach the nozzle by unscrewing (the water will stop flowing).
2 Press nozzle on table-top to free the anti-splash device that is at the bottom of it, or push it out with a pencil.
3 Lever the washer-jumper out from the anti-splash device, brush the latter clean, and put in a new washer-jumper.
4 Put the anti-splash back in the nozzle and screw the nozzle back in place until almost closed (water will start to flow again). Tighten nut, then close the nozzle completely.

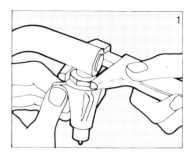

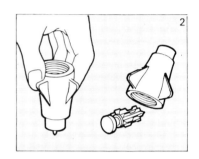

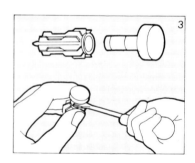

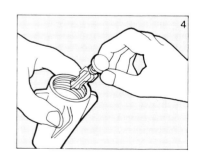

Taps and stopcock – leaking or stiff

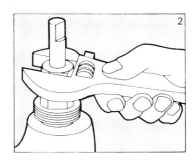

Symptoms
Leaking round the spindle
Tap or stopcock hard to turn on and off

Cause
Any of these may be due to deteriorated
gland packing, or loosened gland-nut.
(Gland packing in a tap may be affected by
water forced back into the tap by a hose
connected to it; or by detergent having
entered from the top and washed the grease
out of it.)

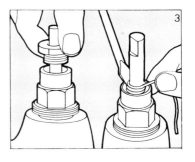

Tools and materials needed
Small screwdriver
Spanners
New gland packing (i.e., string or wool,
and Vaseline)

Method
1 With the tap fully on, remove the handle
  and tap cover (see page 17).
2 Turn the gland nut (at top) clockwise half a
  turn, using a spanner. Test, and if this has
  not ended the leak, try another half-turn.
3 If this does not solve the problem, remove
  the nut completely, pick out the packing
  and replace it with new string smothered in
  Vaseline. Wind this round two or three
  times (do not over-stuff) and press it down
  with the screwdriver tip.
4 Reassemble the tap.

Symptom
Stopcock leaking. (This should be repaired
without delay, for fear of dry rot.)

Method
Repair in the same way as a tap – see page
17. In the case of a main stopcock, the water
authority should be asked to cut off the
water supply to the house – or to do the
repair for you.

Note Some modern taps have a plastic O-
ring on the spindle instead of gland
packing; this is easier to replace than
string.

Taps – replacement

Tools and materials needed
New tap
Washers (see below)
Spanner
PTFE tape

Method
1 Having drained the water supply (see pages 11–12) remove the old tap by undoing the pipe and the nut below the basin. (If these are so awkwardly situated that an ordinary spanner will not reach, obtain a special basin wrench as shown in the diagram.)
2 If the new tap is to go on a ceramic basin, place the washers above and below the ceramic before securing the tail of the tap with a nut.
3 If it is to go on an enamel or steel sink or bath, it will need one ordinary and one 'top hat' washer, the latter to be fitted below the enamel rim as shown; secure tail with nut.
4 Before securing the nut which joins the pipe to the tail of the tap, wind PTFE tape clockwise round the screw-thread of the tail.

Note You can get extra-long tap connectors, which are easier to install. These plastic connectors need no sealing round the thread.

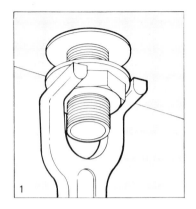

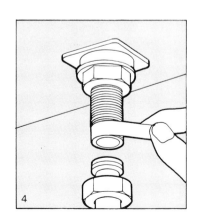

Water-pipes – leaking

Cause
Crack, insecure joint

Tools and materials needed for cracks
Hammer (for lead pipe)
File or abrasive paper
Special tape or filler: see below
Spanners (for insecure joints)

Methods for cracks
The following are a choice of temporary measures, to use after draining the system (see pages 11–12). Usually a cracked pipe will need to be replaced in due course.

1 **First aid** A small crack can be sealed for a short period by rubbing soap into it and tying a rag round; or by tying with a rag saturated in paint, Vaseline or something greasy; or by securing with plastic sticky-tape or a waterproof sticking plaster. Many of the fillers and tapes mentioned on page 15 will seal a crack. If the split is in a lead pipe, it can be hammered together. Restore water supply gently and at low pressure.

2 **Epoxy resin** This type of adhesive filler gives a more durable repair. Rub the surface with a file or abrasive paper, mix the resin in accordance with the maker's instructions, and smear over and round the crack. Bind a glassfibre or other bandage round and smear more resin over this. Leave to set before restoring water supply.

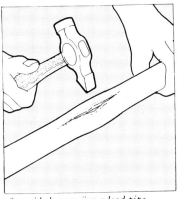

first aid: hammering a lead pipe

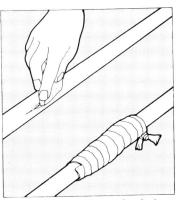

first aid: filling with soap, bandaging

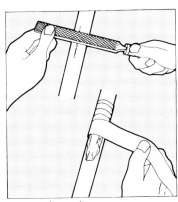

epoxy resin repair

3 **Epoxy putty** is an even simpler
alternative. This comes in two parts which
need to be blended together by repeatedly
rolling, breaking up and kneading before it
is applied. It can then be smoothed down
by wiping with a damp cloth smeared with
soap. A very shiny surface is left if the
putty is covered with polythene (from a
plastic bag) while setting.
4 **Plastic steel** is specifically for pipes:
epoxy plus steel particles.
5 **Pipe seal** is a special two-part tape, giving
a permanent seal. Wind the impregnated
tape round the pipe (or hose), then the
reinforcing tape, and then more of the
impregnated tape.

Notes
1 Neglected leaks can start rot in woodwork.
2 If water leaks into electrical fittings, there
is a danger of shock: turn off electricity
main switch.

Method for joints
Compression joints (those assembled
with nuts). Using spanner, tighten nut
from which water is leaking. Grip the body
of the fitting or the pipe very firmly (with
spanner, vicegrip, etc.) to avoid loosening
other nuts.
Soldered joints Treat like leaking pipe,
or call in plumber to replace joint.

Water-pipes – frozen

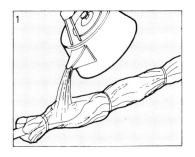

Tools and materials needed
Boiling kettle and cloths; or hair drier, fan
heater, blow-lamp (not on plastic pipes)
etc.; or hot water bottles; or candles.
Salt (for waste-pipes)

Methods
1 Apply warmth to the frozen pipe wherever
  it is accessible; the heat will travel along
  the pipe to other parts. Start near tap,
  turned fully on, or near other outlet from
  which melting ice can escape. (If in doubt
  which part of the pipe is frozen, turn each
  tap on in turn and observe which ones run
  dry.)
2 In the case of waste-pipes and WC, put salt
  in to thaw the ice, followed by boiling
  water.
   Watch out for possible leaks as the ice
  thaws.

Water-pipes – noisy – poor flow

Symptoms
Hammering or other noise
Poor flow

Cause
Faulty gland packing in a tap (see page 21);
or faulty ball-float (see page 28). In the case
of poor flow, a stop-cock may not be fully
turned on. Some noises are due to pipes
being inadequately secured to joists or
walls.

Water-pipes – air-lock

Symptom
Erratic flow from tap, often with hissing and spluttering

Cause
Air-lock (trapped bubbles)

Tools and materials needed
Hosepipe and tap-connectors or clips

Methods
1 Connect one end of the hose to a cold tap served direct from the rising main (usually, only the kitchen tap) and the other to the affected tap. If the kitchen cold tap is inconvenient, connect to any other tap. Turn both full on, and the pressure of the water should blow the bubble out. It helps to turn on other taps that are on the pipe-run that has the blockage. If it is a hot pipe, it helps to stop up the overflow pipe that goes from the hot system into the cold tank. (If air-locks occur often, a plumber can fit an air-release lock.)

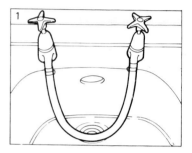

2 Alternatively (unless the air-lock is in a hot pipe), push a piece of hosepipe into the outlet of the cold tank and, with all cold taps turned on (except the kitchen one), blow down the hose.

3 If neither of these methods will do, drain the water system (see pages 11–12). Then close each tap two-thirds before turning the water-supply on again. When all are flowing gently and equally, turn each tap on a little more (lowest ones first), then a little more again. Turn off equally gradually and in the same order.

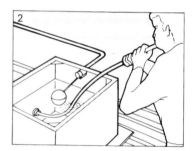

Water tanks – rust

Symptom
Rust traces (in the water supply or in the tank)

Cause
Corrosion of the galvanized steel tank

Tools and materials needed
Wire brush or abrasive paper
Goggles (or eye protectors, sold by opticians, to clip on spectacles) if using wire brush
Rust-killer and steel wool
Possibly epoxy filler or plastic steel
Odourless bituminous paint or zinc paint (these are suitable only for cold-water tanks, not hot)
Paintbrush (or soft broom)
File (if zinc paint is used)
Brush cleaner or white spirit

Method
1 Drain tank (see pages 11–12).
2 Dry it, and remove all loose rust with a wire brush or abrasive paper (wear goggles if you use a wire brush).
3 Coat with rust-killer, rubbed on with a steel wool pad and left to soak for 10 minutes.
4 If the tank is deeply pitted, apply epoxy resin (see page 23).
5 Apply two coats of bituminous paint. Alternatively, use zinc paint. The latter involves filing bare some patches of the steel, dabbing the paint on and, after 10 minutes, painting it liberally everywhere. After $\frac{3}{4}$ hour, splash water lightly all over. Restore the water supply when the paint is dry, about 1 to 2 days.
An alternative is to line the tank with a flexible plastic liner.

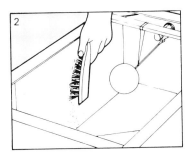

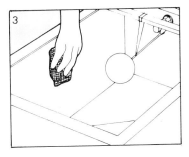

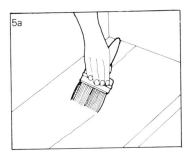

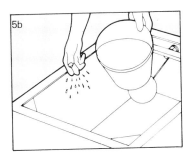

Water tanks – overflowing

Cause
Faulty ball-float; or deteriorated ball-valve washer

Tools and materials needed
Possibly new ball float (plastic)
Pliers
Possibly new washer, screwdriver, Vaseline, and steel wool for cleaning

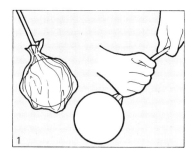

Method
1 Unscrew the float and shake it: if you hear water inside, it is leaking and needs replacement. To keep water from entering the tank or cistern until the new float is screwed on to the arm, tie the arm to a piece of wood lying across the top of the tank as shown left. Alternatively, enlarge the hole, shake the water out and – after screwing the float back – tie a plastic bag round it. If there is no leak, adjust the float arm: bending it down (gently) will shut off the water supply at a lower level. (A few have an adjustable nut on them.)

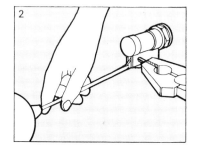

2 If overflow continues, cut off water supply (see pages 11–12) and use pliers to remove the split pin holding the arm. If the pin looks worn, replace it. In the case of a WC cistern, you may have to remove the flush-handle first in order to get at it. Coax the arm out of the slot in the valve.

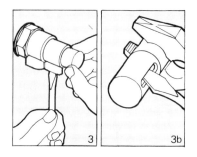

3 Unscrew the cap at the end, if there is one, and slide the plug out with the help of a screwdriver if necessary (there is a slot in it for this purpose). Tapping gently round the end with a hammer may help.

4 Unscrew the two halves (you may need to apply hot water or a release lubricant) and put a new washer in. (Rather than damage the plug while forcing it apart, it may be better to pick out the old washer with a penknife and squeeze the new one in.)

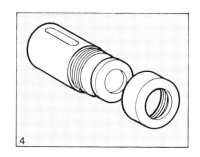

5 Clean and grease the plug and the inside of the valve, before re-assembly.

Water tanks – slow refilling

Cause
Possibly, scale or grit in ball valve

Tools and materials needed
Pliers
Screwdriver
Vaseline

Method
As for rewashering ball-valve (see page 28).
If this is ineffective, a plumber may need to
put in a different type of valve. Some old-
fashioned ball valves can be replaced
completely with diaphragm valves, less
likely to go wrong.

Cisterns – noisy refilling

Materials needed
Silencer pipe (a short tube with a screw
end)
Vaseline

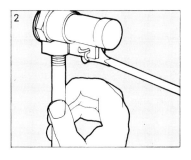

Method
1 Tie up the arm of the ball-float (see page
  28) and flush the WC to empty the cistern.
2 Grease the screw-thread and screw it into
  the hole that is beneath the ball-valve.
3 Release the arm.

Cisterns – noisy flushing

Cause
Old valve

Tools and materials needed
Float valve
Spanner
Scissors

Method
1 Having drained off the water (see pages 11–12) and unscrewed the old valve, pass the connector of the new valve through the hole in the cistern, in order to hand-screw it to the inlet pipe (with washer between pipe and cistern). Check that the polythene tube of the valve is hanging straight down, then tighten the nut with a spanner.
2 Snap the rod of the float on to the float-arm. (The rod length can be adjusted after the water is restored, and any surplus cut off.)
3 Restore the water supply and check whether the valve operates properly when the WC is flushed. (If, after repeated operation, it fails to close properly, the cause is likely to be debris from the cold-water system. Open up the valve and clean it out.)

Other noise-reduction methods
Put rubber sleeves round screws fixing WC cistern to wall. Put resilient draught strips round and under WC door, and panel both sides of it.
Box in waste-pipes with thick chipboard, sealing all gaps, but leave space between boards and pipes. Pipes should not fit too tight in clips or holes; nor be so loose that they vibrate against hard surfaces (use resilient padding, polyurethane foam, or something similar to cushion them).

Cisterns – failure to flush

Cause
Water level too low; or deteriorated valve in the siphon

Tools and materials needed
Spanner
Siphon flap-valve

Method
1 If the water level is more than 10mm below the overflow pipe, detach and bend the arm of the ball-float up a little.
2 If the water level is correct, tie up the float arm (see page 28) and flush the cistern to empty it.
3 Disconnect the flush pipe, unscrew the nut below the cistern, and lift out the siphon.
4 Replace old valve as shown.
5 Reassemble and release float arm.

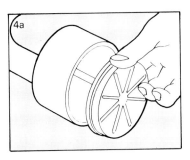

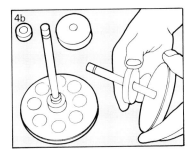

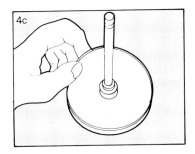

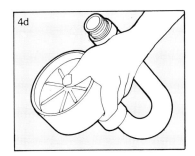

Cisterns – condensation

Symptom
Drips from exterior of cistern

Cause
Condensation due to inadequate
ventilation in the room

Tools and materials needed
Anti-condensation paint, paintbrush and
brush cleaner (or white spirit)
Or foam strips (as sold for condensation
that runs down windows and on to sills)
Or polystyrene (as sold for lining walls)
Sandpaper, scissors and waterproof
adhesive

Method
1 **Anti-condensation paint** (This is
suitable only for iron cisterns, not ceramic
ones. It is often sold by ship's chandlers.)
Paint on in the usual way, then finish with a
stippling action. It has a textured look
because it contains cork granules. After a
day, it can be painted (its natural colour is
off-white).
2 **Foam strips** Stick round bottom of
cistern to catch the drips.
3 **Polystyrene** Drain cistern (see page 30)
and after glasspapering inside it, glue
polystyrene on. Dry overnight.

Symptom
Overflowing – see Water tanks, page 28
Slow refilling see Water tanks, page 29

WCs – uneven flush

Cause
Obstruction; or tilting of pan

Tools and materials needed
Spirit level
Screwdriver
Dryish mortar made with 1 part cement to
3 of sand (or buy ready-mixed mortar)
Grommets

Method
1 Check that nothing is obstructing water
  inlet or rim (a mirror will help you see
  under this).
2 If the spirit level shows the pan is not level,
  loosen the screws fixing it to the floor.
  Remove those on the side that is to be
  raised.
3 Raise this side with scraps of board until
  the spirit level shows the pan is straight.
4 Pack mortar below. Replace screws loosely,
  with grommets (sleeves) round them, and
  screw tight three hours later.
  Warning Do not attempt this if pan is
  rigidly fixed to an iron waste-pipe; you
  might crack the joint.

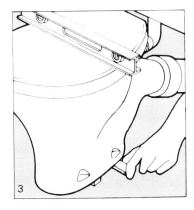

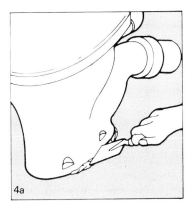

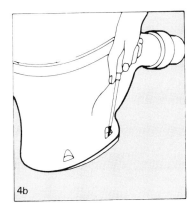

WCs – seat and lid replacement

Tools and materials needed
New seat and lid set (tell retailer the size of
the bolt holes in the WC, and their distance
apart)
Pliers
Screwdriver

Method
Undo nuts fastening old seat to WC, and
remove it. Follow manufacturer's
instructions for assembling and fixing new
set. Do not over-tighten wing nuts.

Note A break in a plastic seat or its hinge
can be repaired with epoxy putty (see page
15).

Bathroom fitments

Cracks, chips
(in basins, baths, sinks, WCs)

Temporary repairs can be made with
waterproof sticky tape on the underside of
cracks; or cracks and chips can be
permanently filled with epoxy putty (see
page 15). Allow time for drying before
running any water on. Use bath enamel to
paint the repair (several coats). Some bath
manufacturers supply their own filler for
repairs.

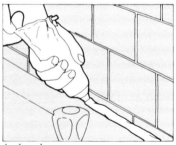

bath sealant

press-in sealant strip

Gaps at wall
(round basins, baths and sinks)

As a hard-setting filler would probably
crack, use a flexible and waterproof bath
sealant, preferably made of silicone rubber.
Clean off all soap traces first, and squeeze
the sealant well inside the gap.
Alternatively, to fix outside the gap, use
special plastic tape supplied with contact
adhesive, or press-in sealing strip (see page
15).

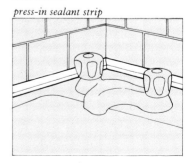

Showers

Symptom
Continual dripping

Cause
Deteriorated O-ring (a kind of washer)

Tools and materials needed
Screwdriver
O-ring

Method
Having turned the water supply off (see pages 11–12) unscrew the flexible hose.
Unscrew the shower-diverter.
Beneath this is a connector with a slot: holding screwdriver in this slot as shown, push the connector off.
Pull out the mechanism from the body of the tap, slide off the old O-ring, and put a new one on.

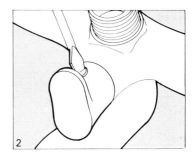

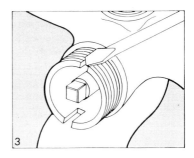

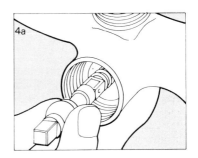

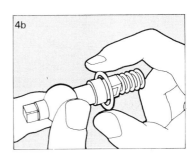

Showers

Symptom
Reduced flow

Cause
Scale in shower-head or mixing valve

Tools and materials needed
Descaling powder or liquid
Or vinegar

Method
Unscrew affected parts and soak for an
hour in $2\frac{1}{4}$ litres (4pt) of nearly boiling
water to which the powder has been slowly
added, or in descaling liquid or vinegar.

Water heaters – electric immersion

Symptom
Water too hot or cold; slow reheating

Cause
Thermostat wrongly set
Possibly, scale from hard water

Tool needed
Screwdriver

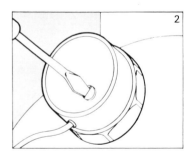

Method
1 Turn off electricity.
2 Undo screw holding the cover.
3 Prise off cap covering the regulator.
4 Use screwdriver to turn screw that
  regulates the setting; 60°C (140°F) is
  normal in hard water areas, 70°C (160°F) in
  soft water areas.

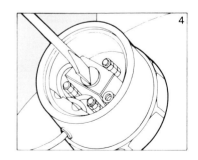

Water-heaters – gas

Symptom
Pilot flame inadequate

Cause
Wrongly adjusted, or clogged

Tools and materials needed
Small screwdriver
Primus pricker

Method
1 Remove front of casing (pull off control knobs first if necessary).
2 Use screwdriver to adjust the screw on the pilot while it is alight.
3 If the jet is blocked, turn pilot off and use the pricker to clear it.
4 Reassemble and, after lighting pilot again, wait 5 minutes before using the water heater.

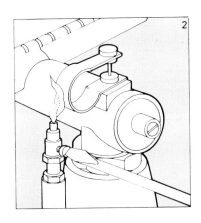

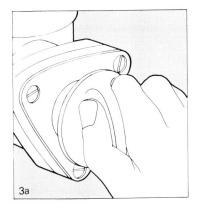

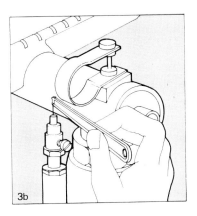

Water-heaters – gas

Symptoms
Poor flow or not hot enough; drips from spout

Cause
Possibly, scale from hard water (removing this in a *large* heater is a job for a gas serviceman)

Tools and materials needed
Rubber tube
Plastic funnel
Descaling fluid

Method
1 Turn off water and gas supplies.
2 Disconnect water inlet, and in its place attach about a metre of rubber tube.
3 With end of tube held above top of heater, pour fluid into it through the funnel – very slowly to prevent it foaming back.

Symptom
Burners fail to light when water is turned on, or light feebly

Cause
Possibly, metal strip by pilot light is not functioning; or gas filter needs cleaning; or gas pressure needs increasing (see also Pilot flame inadequate page 37)

Tools and materials needed
Screwdriver
Possibly new bimetallic strip

Methods
Check that control knob or lever is fully in 'on' position; and that gas main tap is fully on.
Metal strip
1 Press strip down with screwdriver tip (with pilot light on). If burners now light, this means strip is at fault. Turn off gas and put

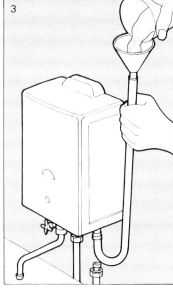

pouring descaling fluid into heater

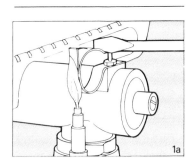

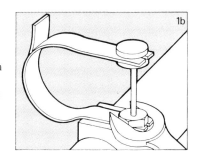

in a replacement (loosen the nut to free the old one from the pin).

2 Alternatively, if strip is not at fault, press pilot fitment gently nearer to the strip so that its flame can make contact.

3 If the pin holding the metal strip is too tight, turn off gas and work it up and down repeatedly to loosen it.

Filter

4 Look for this on gas inlet pipe. Undo cover; take out and clean filter; reassemble.

Pressure

5 Look for governor on gas inlet pipe. Remove cover and adjust screw till pressure increases. One cause of low pressure can be rust flakes in old pipes: the gas authority can vacuum these out (no charge).

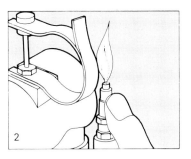

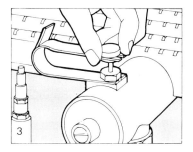

Symptom
Lights with sudden roar

Cause
Build-up of gas before pilot lights the burners

Tool needed
Screwdriver

Method
With gas off, gently bend pilot fitment nearer to burners.

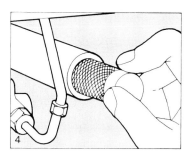

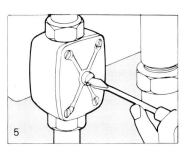

Water heaters – gas

Symptom
Smell of burnt gas when in use (this is dangerous)

Cause
Blockage in ventilation duct (or running a small unflued heater for more than 10 minutes)

Method
1 Hold a match under the cowl while the water heater is on. If this goes out, it may be because the burnt gas is coming back into the room.
2 Check from inside and outdoors whether duct is blocked by, for instance, a bird's nest which you can remove. If this is not the cause, call gas service.

testing for blockage

Symptom
Leaks from joints

Cause
Loose nuts

Tools and materials needed
Spanner
Vaseline
Possibly washers

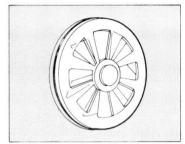

window fan

Method
Grease and then tighten (but not too much), replacing any worn washer.

Note Any room containing a small unflued heater should be well ventilated. One simple method is to drill a row of holes through both a window-frame and a door to ensure a current of air, but window-ventilators or airbricks are neater.

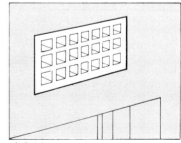

air brick

Boilers – descaling

Symptom
Poor flow of hot water; sometimes with gurgling, hissing and knocking sounds

Cause
Scale from hard water (you can check whether this is the cause by seeing whether your kettle, too, has scale in it)
Descaling pipes or a hot water cylinder is a job for a plumber; descaling a boiler can be done by an amateur

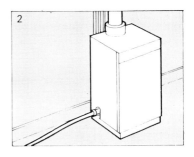

Tools and materials needed
Method A
Boiler descaler (6kg for an average boiler)
Hired descaling unit
Hose and clips
Method B
Boiler and central heating kit
Method C
Liquid descaler for central heating systems

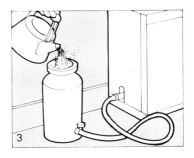

Method A
1 Turn off or rake boiler out. Drain hot water system (see pages 11–12).
2 Check that the drain cock on the boiler has no leak (if it has, the washer must be renewed before proceeding further) and connect tube of descaling unit to it.
3 Pour into the unit 1kg (2¼lb) of the descaling powder and add 1 litre (2pt) of nearly boiling water; shake to mix.
4 With the unit standing 2 metres (6ft) above the floor, turn its tap on so that the fluid flows into the boiler via the drain cock.
5 Repeat this operation until 3kg (6½lb) of the descaling powder has been used and then wait 3 hours or until the liquid is motionless and silent (it gurgles while it is active).
6 Repeat steps 3 to 5 with the remainder of the powder.
7 Restore the water supply and flush the system clean for fifteen minutes by means of a hose connected to the drain cock and leading to an outdoor gulley.

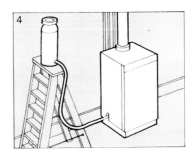

Boilers – descaling

8 Turn off the drain cock and disconnect the hose. After refilling and lighting the boiler, run hot water from all taps until the water is free of all colour.

Method B
1 Switch off boiler and turn off water supply to boiler tank. Drain the boiler, wearing rubber gloves.
2 Pour descaling liquid into the tank, then turn the water supply on again.
3 Switch boiler on again and run at low temperature for 3 hours.
4 Turn off water supply, drain boiler.
5 Dissolve neutralising crystals in hot water and add to tank.
6 Turn on boiler for 15 minutes, drain, flush with clean water.
7 Close drain cock, fill with water.

Method C (central heating system)
1 Drain the hot water system.
2 Fully open radiator valves and vents.
3 Add the acid to the header tank while it refills with water (allow $4\frac{1}{2}$ litres [1 gallon] of special descaler for every 90 litres [20 gallons] of water in system and for every 5 years of its age).
4 With temperature control at 65°C (150°F) leave to circulate for 2 days. (Repeat steps 3–4 if system needs more than $4\frac{1}{2}$ litres [1 gallon] acid per 90 litres [20 gallons] water.)
   Alternatively, in summer, circulate cold for a week, then turn heat on for 6 hours only.
5 Drain and rinse three times as follows: tie-up ball-valve in header tank and drain the hot solution out with radiator vents closed, release ball-valve and refill with cold water, then re-open vents. Drain, then bail out any water left at the bottom of the tank.
6 Refill.

Note When the system is clean, corrosion inhibitor can be put in to prevent future trouble.

Waste-pipes – blockage

Symptom
Water unable to flow away, or flowing
sluggishly

Cause
Blockage from solid matter and/or grease.
Avoidable causes include: flushing
disposable paper goods down WC;
allowing hairs from shampooing to go into
washbasin drain; pouring fat or cooking oil
down sink drain; failing to add a sink-
strainer to drain-hole or to use sink-tidy for
food scraps.
For frozen waste-pipes, see Waterpipes,
page 25.
For main drains, see pages 49–50.

Tools and materials needed
Alternatives, depending on method
chosen, include: washing soda, caustic
soda, spirits of salts, flex or steel-tape
drain-clearer; plunger: large spanner and
bucket; hosepipe and clip or connector.
Some waste-hole grids can be removed
with a screwdriver.

Alternative methods
1 **Boiling water and washing soda** may
clear minor blockages.
2 **Caustic soda** (sodium hydroxide) can be
used in jelly form to dissolve material
blocking WCs. First, bail out as much of
the trapped water as you can. Empty the tin
into a gallon of cold water, stir well, and
pour slowly in. Leave for an hour before
flushing it away. Repeat if the first
application was ineffective. Caustic soda
crystals are less powerful but adequate for
many sink and basin blockages (and to
clean overflows made smelly by a build-up
of soap–alternatively, use a wire-handled
bottle brush). Having bailed out what
water you can, put 3 tablespoons of crystals
in the wastepipe, followed by a cup of hot
water. Flush away after half an hour. Be
careful not to splash: caustic can damage
textiles, paintwork or aluminium and will
injure skin or eyes. If an accident occurs,

Waste-pipes – blockage

flush the injury with plain or (better still) salt water. Any eye injury should be reported to a doctor immediately. Store the tin out of children's reach. Other chemical solutions for this problem are fluid sold for caravan WCs; or a product sold for cleaning masonry.

3 **A flex drain-cleaner** is similar to curtain flex (from which a drain-clearer can in fact by improvised). It consists of about a metre of spiral wire with one end opened up like a corkscrew. This end is gently inserted into the blocked wastepipe or overflow of a basin or sink, while turning the handle at the other end in a clockwise direction. When the obstruction has been shifted, by pulling more than pushing, continue turning while withdrawing the wire. It may help to use the flex from the other end of the waste-pipe if this is accessible nearby outside the house.

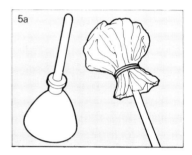

4 **A steel-tape drain-clearer,** also for use in sink or basin waste-pipes, is much longer and can usually penetrate right through to the outside end of the waste-pipe. By pushing and then pulling, while at the same time twisting the tape by means of a grip provided at the other end, the conical front of the tape can be worked past the blockage and then used to free it. Finally, wind it back. A more powerful flexible drain-clearer is obtainable from hire shops.

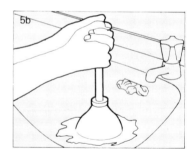

5 **A plunger** consists of a rubber or flexible plastic cup on a handle. Larger sizes have a disc above to spread the pressure on the cup and to prevent it from turning inside out. More expensive pump-type plungers are also sold. A plunger can also be improvised: tie a plastic bag round the head of a mop, or round a sponge tied to a stick; or screw the rubber disc from a power sander to a stick. When using a plunger in a sink, bath or basin, first stop up the overflow with a wet cloth so that air cannot escape this way. Fill the basin, and place the plunger over the waste hole. Pump vigorously up and down. When the pool of water disappears, the blockage has

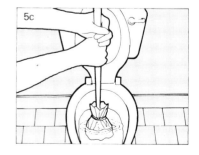

Waste-pipes – blockage

been shifted. In the case of a WC, a long-handled plunger is needed and the action needs to be swift and energetic, but not so vigorous as to crack the pan.

6 **A large spanner** may be needed if it proves necessary to open up the trap in the waste-pipe below the sink, basin or bath. (See advice about spanners and release-lubricants on pages 13–14.) Before starting, place a bucket below the trap to catch water (or a tray in the case of a bath trap) and put the plug in the waste-hole.

U-traps

a Undo the screw-plug at the bottom of the trap using a screwdriver between the lugs, or else using a spanner. Hold the trap steady with the other hand, otherwise you may pull it out of shape. In the case of a bath, you may need an angled bath wrench to reach it.

b If the obstruction does not then clear itself unaided, use a flex drain-clearer inserted from below, directing it into first one half then the other half of the U.

c When screwing the plug back, grease the screw-thread first and do not over-tighten. If its washer is worn, replace it.

Alternatively (where there is no plug at the bottom):

a Use a spanner, if necessary, to undo the two nuts that join the tops of the U to the pipes.

b Use flex to clear the U and the ends of the pipes.

c Screw back carefully – forcing can ruin the screw-thread.

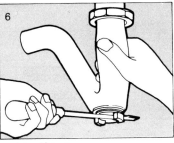

undoing U-trap

clearing U-trap

Bottle-traps
Unscrew the bottom half by hand and poke a flex up into the waste-pipe in both directions.

7 **A short piece of hose-pipe** fastened to a tap can be used to force water into a sink, basin or bath waste-pipe in the hope of clearing the obstruction, but it will be necessary to plug the waste-hole and the overflow with wet cloths as previously described.
   A device which may help when all else fails contains a cartridge of liquid gas which gives a burst of pressure. It can be hired.

Note Do not leave cleared waste-pipes unflushed, for it is necessary to keep their traps filled with water in order to seal off smells from the drains outside.
Occasionally, siphonage keeps on emptying a trap: remedying this is a job for a plumber.
If the blockage is beyond the WC or wastepipe, see Drains, pages 49–50.

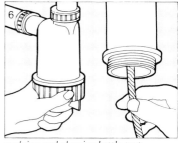

undoing and clearing bottle trap

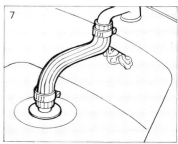

hose-pipe method

Waste-pipes – leaks

Cause
Crack
Or non-watertight joint

Tools and materials needed
Cracks: see Water-pipes
Joints:
Large spanner,
New washer(s),
Vaseline
Or waterproof building tape and non-
hardening sealant

Method
1 **Cracks** See Water-pipes.
2 **Joints** Disconnect (see page 13) and replace
   old washer(s) with new. Grease screw-
   threads before reconnecting.
3 **WC joint** Rake out old filling, bind tape
   round outlet from WC and thrust hard into
   socket, push sealant in, cover with more
   tape.

Typical drainage system

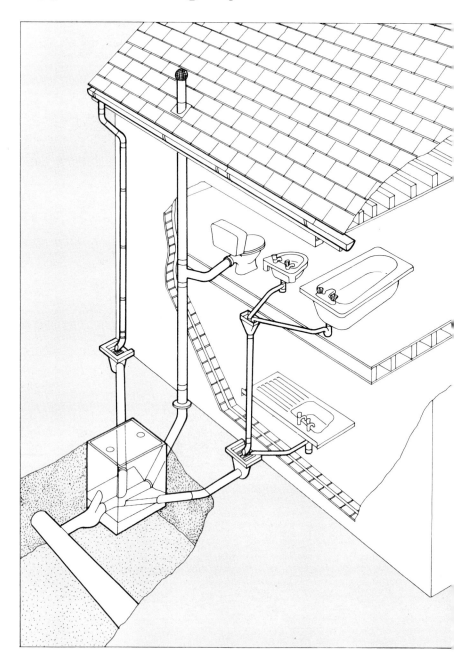

Gulleys and drains

Symptom
Overflowing gulleys

Cause
Blockage

Tools and materials needed
Trowel
Washing or caustic soda
Possibly a new grid
Rubber gloves

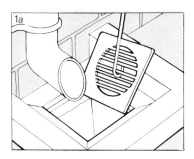

Method
1 If the blockage is in the gulley itself,
remove and clean the grid, and dig any
leaves or debris out. Use washing or caustic
soda as described on page 43, probing with
a stick to help loosen the blockage. Silt at
the bottom is best removed by hand.

2 If the blockage is in the drainpipe below
the gulley, use hired drain-clearing rods
(see overleaf).

3 If iron grid is broken, replace with new
plastic one.

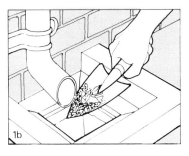

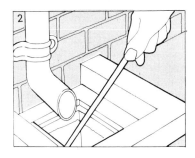

Gulleys and drains

Symptom
Water in drains unable to flow away, or flowing sluggishly. Inspection pit in garden overflowing.

Cause
Blockage

Tools and materials needed
Drain-clearing rods and attachments (from hire shops)

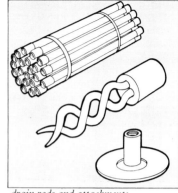

drain rods and attachments

Method
1 Remove cover from pit nearest house. If it has water in it, blockage is further on. Remove cover from next pit if there is one; if this has water, blockage is still further.
   If pits are dry, blockage is within one of the waste pipes coming from the house to the first pit. To identify which one, send water down each in turn and observe which lot fails to reach the pit. (Some houses have only one waste-pipe.)

2 Working from an empty pit, screw the flexible rods together one at a time while pushing them up the pipe that has the blockage. Turn clockwise only, otherwise you will unscrew the rods. The first rod should have the corkscrew attachment on it to loosen the blockage; the rubber plunger is attached instead when pulling is needed.

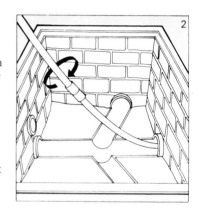

3 If you have to work from a full pit, bail this out to locate the outgoing pipe (centre bottom of the side nearest the road) and try to clear this with the plunger. Failing that you will have to take the stopper out of the 'rodding eye' (a small opening above the outgoing pipe) and push the rod through this. Sometimes it is this stopper that has fallen and is causing the blockage.

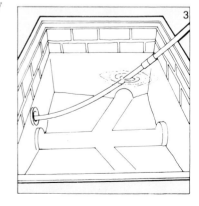

Gulleys and drains

Note Specialized drain-clearing firms using powered rods or pressure jets can be located through the Yellow Pages: ask for a quotation before going ahead, and a guarantee. Alternatively, ask the environmental health department of the local council whether they will clear the drain or recommend a firm. A few councils provide this service free. Jet-operated drain clearers can be hired.

Where a drain serves more than one home its clearance will, if it was laid before October 1937, be treated as a public responsibility though the council may bill the householders concerned for doing it. Shared drains laid since then are the responsibility of the householders concerned. If you call in a drain-clearing firm without prior agreement with others, you will be liable to pay the bill.

Gutters and rainwater pipes

Symptom
Overflows and leaks, stains on wall

Cause
Blockage in gutter; cracks or holes due to rust

Tools and materials needed
Ladder
Stiff brush
Long stick
For cracks: waterproof building tape and scissors
Or waterproof filler

Method
Choose a dry day, without frost.

1 Brush leaves and debris out of gutters.
2 If possible, remove any angled pieces joining gutters to downpipes and clear these out; clear any hopper heads.

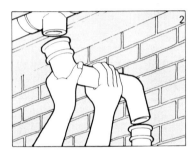

3 Thrust a long stick (with rag tied to its end), or a hose, down pipes. Have a pan ready at the bottom to catch debris.
4 Many cracks can be mended by binding waterproof tape round the pipe or along a gutter (buy an adequate width for the cracks, keep the tape in a fairly warm place, and do not stretch it as you apply it). Clean the suface well first, and overlap the strips of tape (which should extend beyond the actual crack.) Or use a waterproof filler (see pages 23–4) or else a non-hardening mastic.

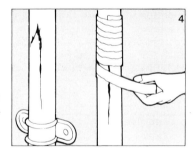

5 If a small part of a gutter has broken off, tie cardboard over the gap, grease the inside and coat thickly with waterproof epoxy filler (let it overlap the gutter by 50mm or more). When it is hard, remove the cardboard.
6 If mesh guards are missing from tops of downpipes, these should be put on. Gutters can be kept free of leaves by clipping on a special gutter grid made of rotproof mesh.

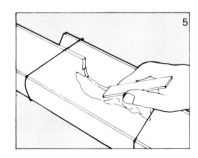

Note There may be gutters not visible from below: between two pitched roofs, or around flat roofs.

Gutters and rainwater pipes

Symptom
Gutters leaking at joints

Cause
Deteriorated sealing material

Tools and materials needed
Ladder
For plastic gutters:
Petrol
New rubber seal
For iron gutters:
Spanner
Screwdriver
Putty
Putty knife
Possibly, hacksaw, bolt, washer and nut

Method
For plastic gutters
(Long sections are usually connected by a short one, called a union, which is lined with sponge rubber seal.)
1 To replace the seal, unclip the union and take it to the retailer to get a new seal of the right size.
2 Use petrol or lighter fluid to clear off all remains of the old seal.
3 Insert the new one and squeeze the gutter ends in order to slip the union back on again.

For iron gutters
(Long sections usually overlap one another and are fastened with a bolt and sealed with putty.)
1 Using a spanner and screwdriver (and possibly dismantling lubricant), remove the bolt.
2 If it is immovable, saw the nut off.
3 Prise the two sections apart and scrape out old putty.
4 Spread new putty in, press the two sections together.
5 Secure with bolt, washer and nut. Alternatively, treat as for cracks, see pages 23–4.

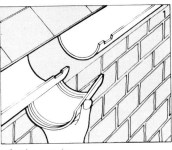

plastic guttering

iron guttering

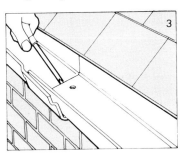

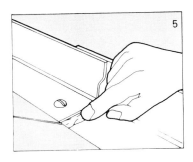

Gutters and rainwater pipes

Symptom
Gutters dripping from middle

Cause
Sagging

Tools and materials needed
Ladder
Bradawl
Screwdriver
Hammer
Large nails

Method
1 Clear out debris that has accumulated in the sag.
2 Lift the sagging section to the correct level again. The gutter should slope slightly but steadily down to the downpipe at one end.
3 It may be necessary to refasten its brackets again in a new position: no problem if they are simply screwed to the fascia board behind the gutter but many are secured to the ends of rafters, inaccessible behind the tiles. Very long nails hammered into the fascia board may give sufficient extra support to prevent the sag recurring, or wedges between gutter and brackets.

Note If the sag is more than about 2cm (1in), rectifying it may break the seal between sections, which will then need renewing as described on page 53.

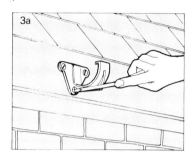

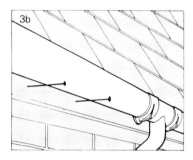

Gutters and rainwater pipes

Symptom
Rainwater pipes leaking from cracks

Cause
Pipe not held securely; or pressure of debris that has entered through unsealed joints

Tools and materials needed
Ladder
Claw hammer
Punch
Epoxy putty
Waterproof mastic filler

Method
To secure a wall bracket that has loosened, remove each section of pipe below the bracket. This is done by unfastening the brackets holding them, using a claw hammer and a piece of wood to lever their nails out as shown. Repair any cracks as on page 15, or buy new section if necessary.

To fasten the wall brackets anew, use a hammer and punch to make large holes in the mortar, fill with wedges of wood and hammer in the nails through the brackets.

Clean any debris out of the pipes before replacing each section, fill the joints with mastic. Do not seal the joints with hard filler – you may want to disconnect them in the future.

Replacement
Because of their light weight and easily clipped on fastenings, plastic rainwater goods are easy to install. Lifting down the heavy old iron ones is the effortful part of the job.

75mm (3in) gutter is usual for sheds, porches and garages; 100mm (4in) for houses. Pipes are 50 or 65mm (2 or 2½in). Only the larger ones are available in black or white as well as grey.

Assemble all the parts on the ground first. Then mark where the gutter brackets are to go on the fascia board (which runs along the top of the wall) and screw these on.

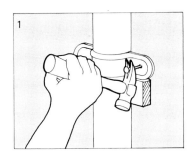

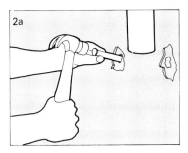

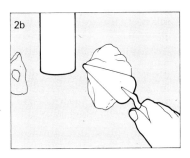

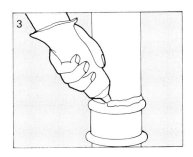

Gutters and rainwater pipes

They should be not more than 1m (3ft) apart; leave no join in the gutter unsupported by a nearby bracket. Some houses have no fascia boards, so special brackets are needed to screw to the ends of rafters under the tiles. The gutter should slope slightly towards its outlet, so nail on a piece of string as a guide before fastening the brackets.

To attach the end outlet to a length of gutter Clip the notched end of the gutter inside the outlet, secured by a gutter strap.
To join two lengths of gutter Clip the end of one inside the other, secured by a gutter strap.
To shorten a length of gutter Use a fine-tooth saw to cut, and a file to make new notches at the sawn end if necessary.
To close the end of a gutter Clip on a stop, secured by a gutter-strap.
To attach a pipe to a gutter outlet An angled pipe, called an offset, is usually needed, pushed on to the end of the outlet. The pipe is then pushed into the offset. If more than one length of pipe is needed to reach the ground, the lengths are simply pushed together.
To secure a pipe to wall Clips encircling the pipe are screwed to plates behind it and these are nailed to the wall. Usually each 3 m (3yd) pipe needs 3 clips.
To terminate the pipe Unless connected to an underground drain, the pipe needs a 'shoe' at the bottom, directing the rainwater into a gulley or water butt.

In addition to these components, there are various clip-on bends and angles for special situations. Downpipe adaptors and waterbutts can be used to conserve rainwater.

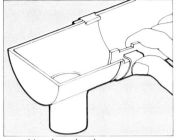

attaching the end outlet

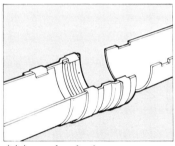

joining two lengths of gutter

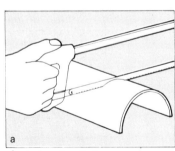

shortening a length of gutter

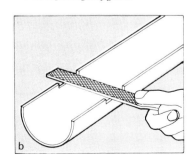

2
Floors and Flooring

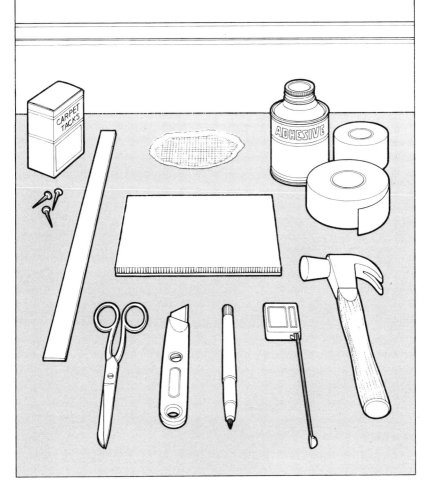

Floor structure

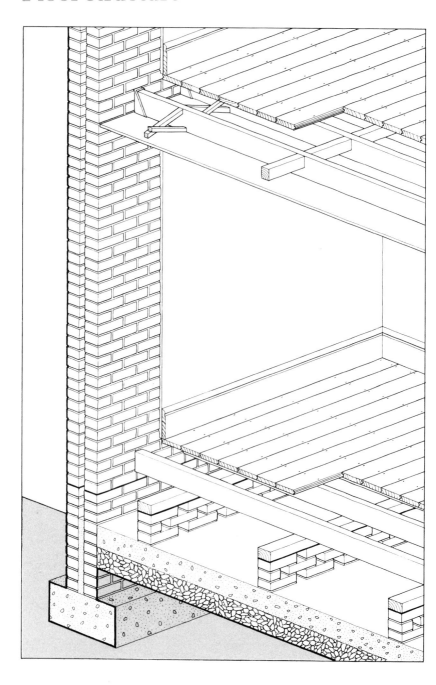

Floor types

The great majority of floors are of either wood or concrete. Other materials used in the past, such as stone flags laid directly on the earth, present special problems if they need attention, and expert advice should usually be sought.

Wooden floors

Wooden floors consist of boards (or, sometimes in modern buildings, sheets of chipboard) nailed to joists. The ends of the joints are supported by various means: dwarf walls built just inside the house walls, steel hangers set into the brickwork, etc., or they are let into the walls themselves. On the ground floor, they have intermediate brick supports; on upper floors, they are deeper and have cross-shaped struts to increase their stiffness.

The edges of the boards are usually tongued-and-grooved both to hold them flat and to stop draughts. Better quality floors are made of narrower boards and superior timber. If meant to be seen, they may be 'secret nailed' so that no nailheads show.

A wooden floor in good condition is warm and comfortable to walk on, and it is easy to lay pipes and wires underneath and to fix most floorcoverings to. It can be sanded and sealed instead of being covered.

But wood can deteriorate, especially in damp conditions. For this reason, it is wise to check the condition of a wooden floor before doing any elaborate and expensive floorcovering job. Examine the boards and skirting against the exterior walls for any signs of rot or damp: if you find any, the woodwork below is likely to be affected. Stand at various points on the floor and bounce with flexed knees: if the floor seems excessively springy, the ends of the joists may have started to rot.

If your suspicions are aroused, take up a board or two so that you can examine the underfloor more closely. One near an outside wall will enable you to check the condition of the ends of the joists, where

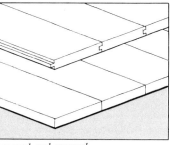

tongued-and-grooved

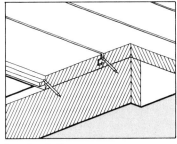

'secret nailed'

Floor types

trouble is most likely. Feel for damp, and press a pointed knife into the wood near the wall: if it goes in too easily, rot has started, and a surveyor or other expert should be called in. A powerful torch or inspection lamp and a small mirror held at an angle of 45° to act like a periscope will enable you to see a long way between joists.

Even with a floor that seems to be in good condition, such an inspection may be worth making if you intend to lay a floorcovering which will not be moved for a long time, especially if it is the ground floor – and see the caution on page 72.

Concrete floors

Though hard and usually cold, concrete floors are durable, and the most serious problem such a floor is likely to present is dampness. This may be present if the concrete was cast over hardcore (compacted rubble) laid directly on the ground, allowing moisture from the soil to soak upwards. This will not occur if there is a damp-proof membrane between the concrete and the screed (the layer of finer material which forms the surface). Such a membrane, of polythene or a bituminous material, is now compulsory in new buildings, but if your home is more than about 25 years old, you cannot count on one being present.

A damp floor may not seem so if it has been covered with a material which has allowed moisture to evaporate as it rose (this includes quarry tiles and parquet), but once an impervious floorcovering has been laid, problems are likely. And a floor can be dry at some seasons but damp at others.

It is not possible to check for dampness without a special instrument, but a rough-and-ready test can be made. Take a piece of waterproof material, such as polythene or foil, and sticky-tape it to the floor round the edges. Leave it for a few days. If there are then signs of wet on the underside, the floor is definitely damp; unfortunately, absence of wetness does not prove that the

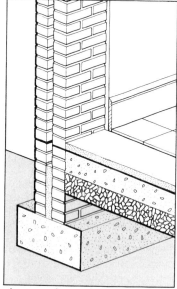

damp-proof course between screed and concrete

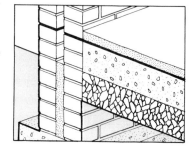

Floor types

floor is definitely dry. (Moisture on the top of the polythene or foil suggests condensation from within the building.) The only floorcoverings that can be laid on damp concrete with any safety are quarry tiles, a few vinyl tiles, and matting of a kind which allows the concrete to 'breathe'.

  The proper solution to the problem is to apply a damp-proof membrane to the concrete in either sheet or liquid form or to lay asphalt. This has to be taken up to meet the damp-proof course in the walls and usually has to be covered with a cement screed. Because of the added thickness, this major job involves trimming doors, re-siting joinery, and so on, and it is one for a builder or specialist firm. But there are proprietary liquids which can be used on top of the existing concrete. They are not the most thorough solution, but if you think they may be an answer to your problem, consult the manufacturers of both the material and the floorcovering you are considering. As a stopgap measure, you can cover the floor with thick polythene stuck down with double-sided adhesive tape.

  Upper floors of concrete, and ground floors not in contact with the soil, should not be affected by damp. But fresh concrete contains moisture, and no impervious flooring should be laid on a newly constructed floor until it has dried out: an allowance of at least one month for each 3cm (1in) of thickness is usual.

Tools

Some tools used for repairing floors and laying floorcoverings are too specialised and expensive to be worth buying for very occasional use. It should be possible to hire them. Among them are the following.

Knee kicker A device for stretching carpet when laying it. Spikes at one end bite into the carpet, and the pad at the other is 'kicked' with the knee while kneeling. It is not needed for laying foambacked carpet.

Flooring saw The curve of the edge makes it possible to cut down into the surface of a wooden floor.

Flooring cramp Used only when laying or re-laying a large area of floorboards, this grips a joist while a screw is turned to tighten a number of boards at once.

Other tools are cheap and versatile enough to be worth buying.

Tack lifter Used for shifting tacks from fitted carpet by levering them from underneath the carpet. Useful for many other levering jobs.

Jemmy or **wrecking bar** With a chisel-like tip at one end and a crook at the other, this greatly eases the removal of floorboards. The crooked end is shaped like the claw of a hammer for pulling out large nails. One about 60cm (2ft) long is convenient.

Nail punches Indispensable for dealing with nailheads. Buy sizes to match the nails to be dealt with.

Straightedge Purpose-made straightedges are available, but a 60cm (2ft) steel rule has more uses, and any straight strip of stiff metal will serve.

Scraper A patent scraper with renewable blades will be needed for stripping and smoothing angles and corners of a board floor which an electric sander will not reach.

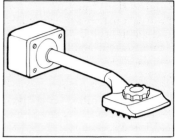

knee kicker

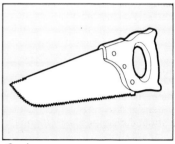

flooring saw

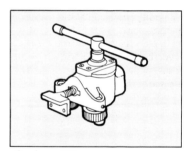

flooring cramp

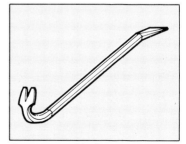

jemmy or wrecking bar

Wooden floors – repairs

Raising floorboards

If you have to raise a floorboard that is in good condition, it is worth going to some trouble to avoid damaging it, so that it can be replaced with minimum trouble and expense. This is particularly true if the floor is to be sanded and sealed, as a damaged board will be unsightly.

Start by looking to see if any boards have been raised and replaced in the past, in case they are in a position which will suit your purpose, as such boards may be easier to get up, especially if they have been re-fixed with screws instead of nails. Likely places are over a central lighting fitting in the room below, and near electric sockets, radiators, etc., which have been installed since the house was built.

Where possible, raise a short board rather than a long one. Long boards which extend under the skirting may be difficult to shift without damaging it and they may have to be cut off short.

Because of the danger of accidentally damaging electric cables under the boards, turn off the electricity at the mains before starting work. This will prevent shocks and short circuits, but proceed with caution nevertheless, especially when using a drill or saw which extends beneath the under-surface of the boards.

Wooden floors – repairs

Tongued-and-grooved boards

Most wooden floors are made with
tongued-and-grooved (t&g) boards. Check
yours by trying to push a thin knifeblade
between two boards: if it goes through
easily, the boards are square-edged.

To raise a t&g floorboard, it is necessary
first to remove the tongues at the sides. (A
board can be simply forced up, but it will
be badly damaged in the process.) With a
short board, cut away the tongues all along
both sides. With a long board, it should be
necessary to cut them away for only 50 cm
(2 ft), as the rest of the tongues should split
off when you start to lever up the board.

Choose one of the following methods
according to the tools available.

Alternative methods

1 Obtain a floorboard saw and, using the
curved side of the blade, cut straight down
into the gap between the boards. Clean grit
out of the crevice first to avoid blunting the
saw.

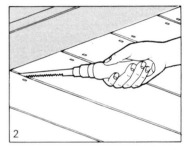

2 Use a narrow-bladed saw, such as the
sawblade of a craft knife, between the
boards. There may be a gap at one end
where you can make a start. Otherwise,
drill a row of small holes next to each other
until you have made a slit long enough to
insert the blade. When the sawcut is long
enough, you can change to a longer saw.
Do not cut into joists (use the saw as
horizontally as possible above them), and
watch out for electric cables and
pipes – feel for them with the back of the
sawblade.

3 Drive a bolster between the boards to cut
through the tongues, working your way
along the length of the board until enough
has split off.

Wooden floors – repairs

Levering boards up

Always lever floorboards from the sides – not the end, which will split. Drive a bolster or other stout tool into the gap with a hammer, starting near the end. Lever the board upwards until it has shifted slightly, then do the same at the other side. Work at each side alternately until you have raised the board enough to get a second tool underneath it. You can then use another lever or the head of a claw hammer to lever the board upwards more vigorously.

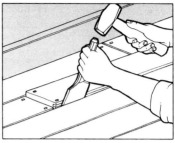
levering up a floorboard

With the nails at the end free, put a piece of wood, etc., under the raised end of the board from side to side, and lever the board as close as you can to the next joist. As the board 'gives', move the wood along, levering as you go, pulling the nails out of each joist in turn. It may help to bear down on the raised end, but not so heavily as to risk snapping the board.

Continue until the whole board is free, or cut it across at right angles at the centre of a joist.

If it proves difficult to make a start when levering up a board, check that the tongues have been completely severed at the end. If they have, try one of the following ways of shifting the end.

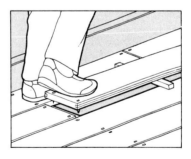

1 About 2½cm (1in) from the end and from the side, drive a thick screw into the board (not through the joist), leaving the head standing above the surface, and use the claw of a hammer or a jemmy to lever up the end until you can carry on in the usual way.

2 Drive the nails right through the board, using a thick punch. (This method can be used for any stubborn nails along the length of the board.)

3 If all else fails, bore a large hole through the board, avoiding the joist, and force the board up with a lever in the hole. This method will involve replacing the end of the board (see page 67).

Wooden floors – repairs

Removing a short length
It is sometimes necessary to raise a short piece in the middle of a board which cannot be removed as a whole – perhaps because the ends are obstructed by fitments.

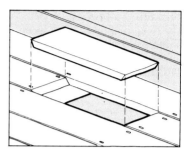

At each end of the piece, cut it through 2½cm (1in) away from the centreline of the joint, which is where the nails will be seen. Use a narrow-bladed saw as in Method 2 on page 64, but incline the saw slightly away from the joist so as to make an angled cut. Saw away the tongues of the boards similarly (cutting through one may be enough). Lift out the cut piece.

To replace such a piece, use two strips of wood at least 5cm by 2½cm (2in by 1in) and longer than the width of the board. Nail or screw these flush with the top of each joist, and nail the piece of board to them.

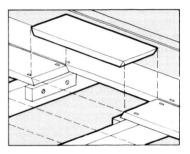

Replacing boards
The best nails to use for floorboards are floor brads. These taper, so that they pull out easily once they have been shifted. But oval wire nails are good enough for small jobs. Use the same length as that of the original nails.

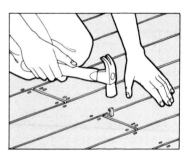

Before replacing a board, pull out any nails left in the joists. Any that will not move can be bent to and fro with pliers until they break, and the stump can be hammered in. Remove nails from the board and brush or scrape all dust from the edges of the boards and the tops of the joists.

Place the new nails alongside the holes left by the old ones. Drive them in vertically to make later removal of the board easier, but where the nails are close to the edge of the joist (as where a board has been cut across), drive them inwards at an angle to avoid splitting the wood.

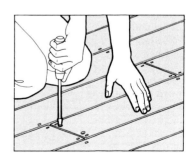

Where a board has started to split, use screws (making starting holes and countersinking them) to avoid making it worse. And use screws where there is any likelihood that you will want to take the board up again – perhaps to get at wiring or plumbing.

Wooden floors – repairs

Replacing a board

A badly split, splintered, warped, or otherwise damaged floorboard should be replaced if the floor is to be sanded and sealed or if it is too uneven to lay a floorcovering on. If possible, use wood of the same thickness for the replacement. This may be difficult to buy new if the floor is old enough to have been made before metric timber sizes became standard: in this case, try to obtain a secondhand floorboard, perhaps from a demolition site. Otherwise use a piece of board which is as close as possible to the right thickness. For the sake of stiffness, it is better for it to be too thick, but a too-thin board will do for a short length and is easier to adapt.

Tools and materials needed

Saw
Shaping tool or plane
Hammer
Nails
Punch
Perhaps scrap plywood or hardboard

Method

Cut the board to the right width, allowing a slight excess so that the sawn edge can be smoothed with shaping tool or plane. Cut it to length. When it fits snugly in place, check the thickness.

Board too thin Pack each joist with pieces of plywood, hardboard, card, etc., until the board is slightly higher than the existing floorboards. (This is to allow for the packing to compress slightly when the board is nailed down.) Tack the packing in position with a small nail in the middle and nail down the board. If it lies slightly above the floor surface, level it with shaping tool or plane after punching in the nails.
Board too thick Mark the position of each joist on the back of the board with a pencil. Make sawcuts about 1cm ($\frac{1}{2}$in) beyond these marks and as deep as the board is thick: do this carefully, as cutting

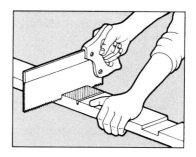

too deeply will weaken the board. Remove
the excess wood with chisel and shaping
tool making frequent checks with the board
in its place. Then nail the board in
position, finally levelling it if necessary
with shaping tool or plane.

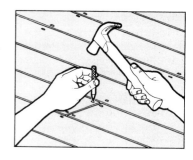

Loose board

Tools and materials needed
Hammer, punch, and nails
Or screwdriver, drill, and screws

Method
Drive home all existing nails and punch
them below the surface. If this does not
work, drive an extra nail into each joist. Or
use screws, especially if the board is
beginning to split; countersink them.

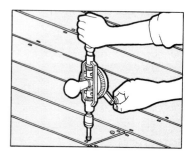

Squeaking board
Squeaking is caused by a board rubbing
against the next one or on a joist or by a
loose nail. So tackle it by securing the
board as described above. If the board still
squeaks, try one of the following.
1 Drive a short, thick countersunk screw
   between the boards to jam them together.
2 Insert talcum powder between the boards,
   using a folded piece of paper, to act as a
   lubricant; or use a puffer pack of powdered
   graphite.

Gaps between boards
Gaps between floorboards occur when the
wood has dried out and shrunk since the
floor was laid. They can be a nuisance for
any of three reasons: draughts, more likely
with square-edged than with t&g boards;
appearance, important only if the floor is to
be sanded and sealed; and unevenness,
which makes it difficult to lay many
floorcoverings and causes uneven wear
thereafter. In the last case, the answer may
be to cover the whole floor with hardboard

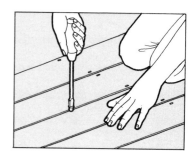

Wooden floors – repairs

(see pages 71–2), but if gaps are not widespread and the floor is generally in good condition, they can be filled. A more drastic solution is to take up all the boards and re-lay them.

Re-laying floorboards

Raise one board (see page 63), then lever up the rest, damaging them as little as possible and stacking them in such a way that they can be replaced in the same order. Scrape dust from edges of boards and tops of joists and remove nails.

Replace the boards a few at a time, cramping them together tightly with a pair of flooring cramps before nailing. Lever the last board tightly into position and fill the remaining gap with a length of suitable wood cut and planed to fit closely.

Filling gaps

Start by picking the dirt out of the gaps (though tight-packed dirt can be an effective filler).

For a large gap, use a length of wood shaped to a slight taper. Coat it with adhesive and hammer it into the gap. When the adhesive is hard, level the wood with a plane or shaping tool.

For narrower gaps, use either newspaper boiled to a pulp and with water-based adhesive added, or wood filler in a colour to match the boards if they are to be seen. Work the filler well down into the cracks, leaving it slightly too high, and sand it smooth when it is hard.

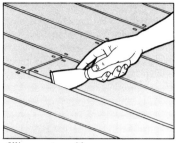

filling a gap – wide

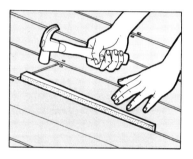

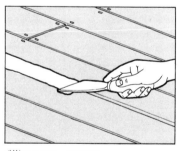

filling a gap – narrow

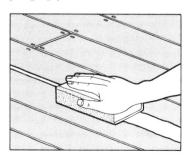

Wooden floors – repairs

Irregularities

Any surface irregularities in a wooden floor should be put right: if the boards are visible, they are unsightly, while even if hidden, they may damage any floor-covering laid on top or make it wear prematurely.

Knots Being both harder and less prone to shrink than the rest of the wood, these may stand above the surface of the floor, especially an old and well-worn one. Do not try to level them with abrasive paper, which will have more effect on the surrounding wood and so make matters worse. Instead, use a plane or shaping tool or sharp chisel.

Nailheads If these are standing up because of wear or because the boards have shrunk since they were laid, they should be hammered level or, preferably, punched just beneath the surface. If the boards are to be exposed, fill the holes left after punching with a coloured wood-filler. Make sure there are no old tintacks round the sides of the room: use a tack-lifter and pincers on them.

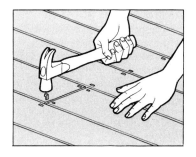

Warped boards Warping is more likely to have occurred with square-edged than with t&g boards, making the sides of the boards stand up. Level them with plane or shaping tool, working across the grain for speed if appearance is unimportant. It is sometimes effective to take up a warped board and replace it upside down, using extra nails to help to flatten it.

Splintering If an old board has developed a splintery surface, try glueing the loose pieces back: use a wood adhesive, cover the area with sheet polythene, and weight it down until the adhesive has set. Or take the board up and replace it upside down.

Surfacing with hardboard

Hardboard can be used to give a smooth, level, and draughtproof floor surface. It is advisable to use it on wooden floors before most of those floorcoverings which are stuck down, both to make adhesion more successful and to prevent uneven wear. For this purpose it is generally laid rough side up, but check the directions for a particular material.

'Exterior' or 'tempered' hardboard should be used in damp places such as kitchens. This type can itself serve (smooth side up) as a floorcovering: finish it with a suitable coloured or clear floor seal.

Use 3mm ($\frac{1}{8}$in) hardboard in 1220mm (4ft) square sheets.

Two days before using the hardboard (three days for exterior board), condition it by wetting the rough side of each square sheet with $\frac{1}{4}-\frac{1}{2}$ litre ($\frac{1}{2}$–1pt) of water, and stacking the sheets with the rough sides against each other. This ensures that the board will shrink and flatten itself rather than swell and buckle.

Tools and materials needed
Hammer
Punch
Tenon saw
Narrow-bladed saw
Hardboard
25mm (1in) ring-shank nails

Method
Sweep floor thoroughly. Hammer or punch in any protruding nailheads. Level any high places (see page 70).

Place first sheet in centre of room (see pages 81–2 for advice on positioning). The edges should not coincide with joins between floorboards. Nail round the sides, placing the nails 1cm ($\frac{1}{2}$in) from the edge and 10cm (4in) apart. Drive more nails in all over the sheet, 10cm (6in) apart each way, starting in the middle.

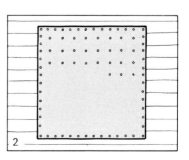

2

Surfacing with hardboard

3 Fix subsequent sheets similarly, working outwards from the central sheet. Stagger the joints in one direction, and pair the nails at the edges of adjacent boards.

4 Trim the sheets for the sides of the room, using a narrow-bladed saw for tailoring. See page 84 for methods of fitting. While being sawn, hardboard should be supported, preferably by a helper, to prevent it from tearing.

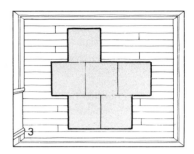

If the hardboard is being laid to serve as a floorcovering, the nails along the edges should be 15cm (6in) apart and those elsewhere 20cm by 40cm (8in by 16in) apart. They should be punched below the surface and the holes filled with a matching wood-filler.

Warning Covering a wooden floor with hardboard (or with any other air-proof material such as building paper or vinyl floorcovering) stops it from 'breathing', and any dampness in the floor or in the space below may be trapped. This can rapidly cause rot in the floor and its supporting timbers. So before doing such work on a ground floor, it is more than usually important to make sure that there are no sources of damp on the outside of the house and that the airbricks are in order. If the space beneath the floor is unventilated, airbricks should be fitted by a builder or – at the least – a floorcovering used which allows some ventilation (see page 61).

Note, too, that any such fixed covering will make it very difficult to get at cables, pipes, etc., below the floor. If necessary, make access panels in the hardboard and screw, rather than nail, them down.

Wooden floors – sanding and sealing

Wooden floors that are in good condition can be sanded and sealed as a cheap and attractive alternative to covering them, though the floor will not be warm soft, or quiet, and the seal may not stand up to very hard traffic indefinitely. Sanding is also a way of smoothing a floor which is to be covered.

Sanding

Sanding needs to be done thoroughly, as any stains, etc., in the boards will be made permanent and conspicuous when the seal is applied.

Very small areas, such as the surround to a carpet square, could be done with an orbital sander or discs used with an electric drill. But most floors will call for a special machine rather like a lawnmower, which is hired. The hire firm will supply abrasive sheets to fit it and charge for them according to the number used.

Before sanding, carry out any repairs needed to the floor (see pages 63–70), though some filling, etc., may turn out to be necessary afterwards. Go over all the boards, punching nailheads just below the surface. If this is not done, not only may the nailheads tear the abrasive sheets, they will also – being harder than the surrounding wood – leave bumps on the surface. For the same reason, use a plane, chisel, or shaping tool on upstanding knots: these may also have to be planed down during the course of sanding as the surrounding wood is abraded away.

Bare boards should present no other problems, but boards which have already been stained may be difficult to sand down to raw wood, so be prepared to use a stain or coloured seal on them so that dark patches do not show up. If wax polish has been used, this should be removed by scrubbing or with white spirit and steel wool, otherwise it will clog the abrasive.

Do as much as you can of the preparatory work before you take delivery of the sanding machine – otherwise you will be

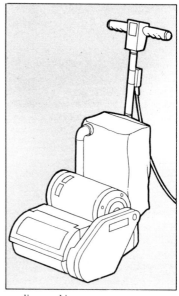

sanding machine

Wooden floors – sanding and sealing

paying for its hire while it stands idle.

Most of the dust from sanding is collected in the bag on the machine, but a lot of fine dust escapes, so the room should be completely emptied and all doors in the house kept shut while the machine is in use. For the same reason, the job should be done in advance of any redecoration. You may want to wear a dust mask, and as the noise can be objectionable, it is advisable to give near neighbours warning.

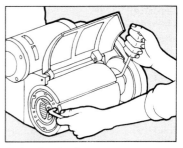

fitting abrasive sheets

The hire firm will show you how to fit the abrasive sheets to the drum of the machine: the ends are fitted into slots in the drum and are gripped by turning simultaneously two keys in opposite directions. If the sheets are very stiff, roll them between your hands.

The coarsest abrasive may be needed only to remove paint or to level very uneven areas. If will be particularly effective if the machine is used at an angle to the boards, when it will remove a lot of wood quickly. But try a medium abrasive first, and avoid sanding to excess: heavy scoring, particularly across the grain, can be difficult to smooth and may show up when the seal is applied, and accidentally grinding away too much wood will make the floor uneven.

sanding floorboards

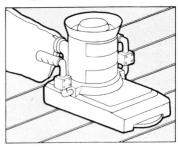

In general, overlap the area just sanded, and finish with the finest abrasive used along the grain. Do not run over the cable – you can drape it over your shoulder.

The machine will not sand right up to the edges of the floor: one side is designed to work up close to the wall (be careful not to damage the skirting), but some areas in corners, etc., cannot be reached. For these you can hire an edge-sander – a heavy-duty disc sander. Or use an electric drill and abrasive discs: hold the drill at such an angle that one side of the disc is in contact with the floor, and keep the disc moving to avoid making circular marks on the floor. Finally, use a patent scraper with renewable blades, followed by hand-sanding with abrasive on a block.

sanding at the edges

Wooden floors – sanding and sealing

Sealing

There is a choice of seals suitable for wooden floors: clear or coloured, matt or eggshell or glossy. For the most natural appearance, stain followed by clear seal may be preferable to a coloured seal, though the time and work involved are greater. Either method is the answer if the floorboards turn out after sanding to vary in colour. Just a pale-shaded stain close to the natural colour of the wood will ensure a more even effect, while a darker material will disguise obstinate discolourations.

At least two coats are usually required. A quick-drying material is obviously preferable. Second and subsequent coats may have to be applied within a certain time, otherwise the previous coat will have to be sanded. Check the directions for a particular brand: the first coat may have to be diluted, and you may need to apply gloss before a last coat of matt or eggshell.

Use a wide paintbrush (at least 5cm [2in]), preferably a new one, as old paint loosened from an imperfectly cleaned one may cause streaks. Or use a lambswool roller.

Vacuum-clean the room thoroughly before starting – avoid making footmarks on the floor. Apply the seal in the direction of the grain, and try to keep a 'wet edge' to avoid overlaps – where you can't, stop at the edge of a board. And work towards the door!

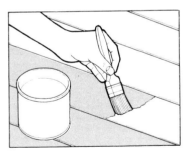

If using a two-pack seal, mix no more than you can use in one session.

Unsealed cork tiles are treated similarly. They need several coats because they are absorbent. Chipboard can be sanded and sealed, as can existing parquet.

Concrete floors – repairs

Cracks and holes

Small cracks and holes in concrete floors are repaired with a cement-based filler, larger ones with sand and cement, which can be bought pre-mixed. If mixing your own, use three parts of sand and one of cement and combine them thoroughly while dry. Make the heap into a volcano-shape and fill the crater with water. Tip material from the sides into the water gradually until all is absorbed, then mix thoroughly.

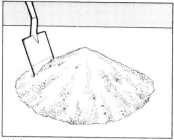

mixing concrete

If the right amount of water has been used, the mixture will hold the marks of a shovel, etc., without collapsing. If it is too wet, sift in sand and cement mixed together and work them in. If it is too dry, add water, preferably with a watering-can fitted with a rose. It is better to use too little than too much water in the first place.

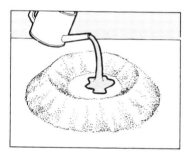

Especially if it is a wide gap with sloping sides that you are filling, add PVA adhesive to the mixing water and paint the sides of the hole with diluted PVA. This will ensure a firm bond and neat junctions (and give a smooth and dust-free surface). Otherwise, wet the sides of the hole.

Use a trowel or steel float to put the cement in place. On a large area, spread it about with a wooden float or broad block of wood, levelling it with a strip of wood from side to side of the hole. A steel float is used to give an extra-smooth surface, but stop before water starts to come to the surface, as this will create a weak and dusty finish.

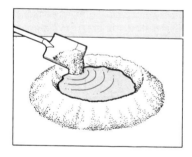

On a hot day, cover a large repair with polythene to stop it from drying too quickly.

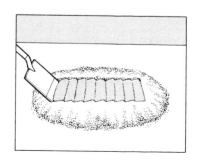

Concrete floors – repairs

Levelling

Most floorcoverings demand smooth and level concrete, free of cracks, pitting, and traces of old repairs. This can be achieved by 'screeding' the whole area with sand and cement, but it is easier to use a special levelling compound.

Such compounds smooth themselves, so no trowel-marks are left, harden quickly, and can be tapered to a 'feather edge' where necessary. They can be used on materials other than concrete, but not on sloping floors. The maximum thickness is 6mm ($\frac{1}{4}$in), so large faults have to be filled as above before levelling compound is used.

Tools and materials needed

Steel trowel
Bucket
Stick for mixing
Levelling compound

Method

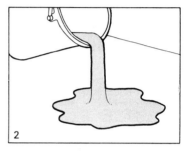

1 Mix powder with water (or liquid supplied, according to brand).
2 Tip some of mixed compound on to floor.
3 Spread over floor with trowel to maximum thickness of 6mm ($\frac{1}{4}$in).
4 Allow to harden before laying flooring (it can be walked on within a hour or two).

Surface treatments

Where a concrete floor is not to be covered, as in a garage or workshop, its surface can be improved in a number of ways.

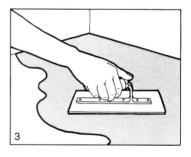

Dustiness, probably the result of badly-made concrete, can be stopped by brushing on a special liquid (the most lasting way), or waterglass (obtainable from chemists), or diluted PVA adhesive.

Seals, of the kind used for wooden floors, will give a more presentable appearance.

Floor paint comes in a range of colours and can be used on other surfaces.

Levelling compound can be left exposed.

Emulsion paint will wear through very quickly but it is cheap and easy enough to renew frequently.

Floorcoverings – selection

The existing floor

Most floorcoverings can be laid on most types of floor, but there are some limitations. When in doubt, consult the manufacturers of the floorcovering.

Damp concrete and stone Unless you can cure the dampness thoroughly or temporarily (see page 61), the only permanent materials to use are some vinyl tiles (which are slightly porous) or quarry or some ceramic tiles. Otherwise use matting such as rush or maize (page 102).

Quarry tiles These may have been laid on a damp basis, so test before using an impervious floorcovering over them (see pages 60–61). Also, they may be uneven and so may have to be levelled with compound (see page 77).

Parquet As this too can 'breathe', it may have disguised the fact that the floor beneath is damp. If parquet has been impregnated with polish over the years, materials which have to be stuck down may not adhere to it. Covering with hardboard or an impervious floorcovering may make the blocks bulge and buckle if they are on damp concrete or an unventilated wooden floor. But parquet can be renovated by sanding and sealing (pages 73–5).

Heated floors These are not suitable for cushioned vinyl, some rubber-backed carpet and carpet tiles, cork, or parquet tiles. Underfloor hot-water pipes laid too near the surface may also cause trouble.

Board floors If smooth, these will take almost any material. The main exceptions are quarry and ceramic tiles unless the floor is strong enough to bear their added weight. If boards have been treated against rot or woodworm, vinyl should not be used on them. And if in doubt about the condition of the floor or the ventilation underneath, see pages 59–60.

Floorcoverings – selection

Old floorcoverings Loose-laid materials
(carpet, lino) should always be removed.
Fixed ones (vinyl tiles, etc.) may have to be
scoured of polish or levelled with
compound (page 77) or both.
Porous materials Bare hardboard,
plywood, or chipboard may need priming
with adhesive before laying self-adhesive
tiles: check the manufacturer's
instructions.

Sheet or tiles?

In many floorcoverings, there is a choice
between sheet or tiles in comparable
materials. Other things being equal, tiles
have the advantage of being easier to lay,
particularly in a room with a complicated
shape, whereas sheet material can be laid
with fewer joins or none – an advantage in
wet conditions as well as for the sake of
appearance.

Check that a sheet material comes in a
width which will not involve excessive
waste. With tiles, check the size against the
dimensions of the room for the same
reason. And, as many tiles are sold in packs
of a certain number, check also that you
will be able to cover the floor without
having to buy a whole pack for the sake of a
single tile. Sizes and packaging differ, so it
might be worth choosing another brand or
even material, though a few spare tiles may
well be useful for future replacements.

Floor coverings – preparation

The thinner and less resilient a
floorcovering is, the more important it is to
lay it on a level and smooth floor.

Wooden floors Carry out any necessary
repair and levelling work (pages 63–70).
Clean the floor thoroughly, and scrub off
any polish with detergent or white spirit,
especially if an adhesive is to be used. Paint
or varnish may have to be stripped.

Concrete floors These too should be
cleaned and repaired (pages 76–7). Any
'nibs' on a new floor should be chipped off.
Very greasy concrete can be cleaned with a
product made for garage floors and
obtainable from some motor-accessory
dealers. If the surface is loose or dusty,
adhesives may not stick (page 77).

Before you start

If cleaning and repairs have made the floor
damp, allow time for it to dry out. And
check the floorcovering manufacturer's
instructions about 'conditioning': most
materials have to be left in the room for a
day or two to acclimatise before they are
laid.

If the new floorcovering will raise the
height of the floor, take down any inward-
opening doors, and trim their bottoms
before replacing them.

Tiles – setting out

With the floor prepared as necessary, start by finding the centre. Tiling should generally be started from this point, not from one of the walls.

Measure two opposite walls and mark the centre of each, ignoring any bays, projections, etc.

Stretch string between drawing-pins at these points, and mark a line on the floor with chalk, using a piece of wood against the string as a straightedge.

Do the same with the other walls.

Check that the two lines are at right angles to each other. An easy way of doing this is to mark points 90cm (3ft) from the centre in one direction and 1.2m (4ft) in the other, and measure the distance between them: if this is 1.5m (5ft), the lines are at right angles (other units of measurement can be used). Redraw one of the lines to get a right angle if necessary.

Starting in one of the angles at the centre, lay out a row of tiles (without fixing them down) as far as you can towards one wall. If the gap which remains is less than about a quarter of a tile-width, you will have to start tiling with the centreline of the middle tile on the centreline of the room.

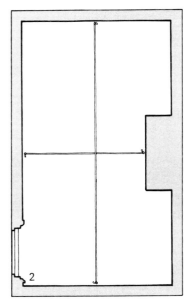

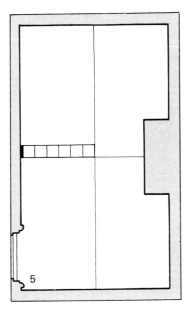

6 Make a similar check in the other direction. There are thus four ways of using the centre of the room as the starting point for tiling while avoiding excessively narrow pieces at the sides (see diagram).

7 If the shape of the room is complicated, lay more tiles 'dry' to make sure that no awkward fitting will be involved.

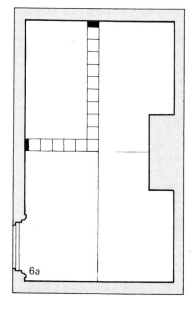

6a

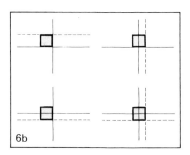

6b

Tiles – laying

With most types of tiles, it is best to lay the first three in an L-shape, beginning at the starting point you have determined as just described. Either continue outwards towards the walls until you can no longer lay a complete tile, and then fill in that quarter of the floor from the centre towards the corner; or work outwards from the centre, making a growing triangle of tiles and then working into the corner.

It is important to lay the first tiles very accurately, as any error here will get worse as you proceed. So take great care at this stage, pushing the tiles up against a straightedge to ensure that they are square and in line.

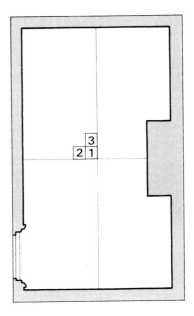

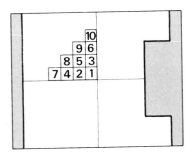

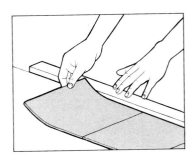

Tiles – laying

Make sure that each tile is the right way round if you are using a material with which this matters: carpet tiles with a nap have to be laid alternately, and other materials with a directional pattern, such as marbled vinyl, look best if the tiles are alternated. You may find arrows on the backs. With patterned tiles, the design may match better on one side than another.

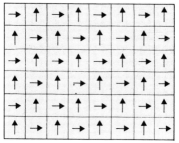

tiles with a nap or a directional pattern should be alternated

Trimming
Some vinyl tiles can be cut with scissors, but for most materials a trimming knife with removable blades is best.

As a rule, cut from the top surface downwards. An exception is carpet tiles, where the backing is cut first. Some of those have a bituminous backing which is slightly tacky: use methylated spirit to clean the knife blade.

Cork tiles need a sharp blade if tearing is to be avoided.

Fitting round the sides
Lay all the tiles you can without cutting. Then tackle those round the sides of the room. For those tiles which are cut from the top, use the following method.

Put a tile (A) exactly on top of the nearest whole tile already laid (B). Place a spare tile (C) so that it overlaps tile A and has one edge firmly against the wall. Either cut or mark tile A, using tile C as a straightedge. One piece of tile A will fill the gap perfectly, the cut edge going against the wall.

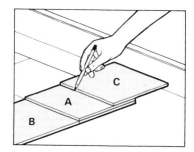

For those materials which have to be cut from the back, turn tile C upside down, overlap it with tile A, and cut or mark it with the edge of tile A. Or use measurements.

Tiles – laying

Fitting round obstructions

To trim tiles to fit such obstructions as pipes and pedestals, it is best to make a template of stiff paper or thin card, having laid as many straightforward tiles as possible. Mark the top of the template if there is any likelihood of confusion, and bear in mind the direction of the tile where necessary.

self-adhesive tile

Application

Smears and spills of adhesive (if used) should be removed immediately, so keep on hand a damp rag or tin of solvent as appropriate.

Vinyl tiles The most popular are now self-adhesive. For other kinds, use an adhesive made or recommended by the manufacturer of the tiles. Using the toothed plastic spreader which is often supplied, cover an area no bigger than can be dealt with while the adhesive remains workable.

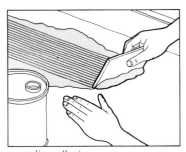

spreading adhesive

Cork tiles Ready-sealed and vinyl-surfaced tiles are generally fixed with a special contact adhesive, bare ones with an emulsion. Avoid marring the surface of the last sort before it has been sealed.

Carpet tiles Though some are described as 'loose lay', these have to be pushed very firmly together to prevent movement. Kneel on the laid area while doing so to prevent buckling. If you are laying an area of more than about 9sq m (10sq yd), every third row in each direction should be stuck down – or more frequently if the floor surface is slippery. Either use suitable double-sided adhesive tape down the middle of the tiles in those rows, or put spots of latex adhesive on the corners of each tile in the row. At a doorway, stick the tiles down and fit an edging strip (page 101). Also stick down tiles round the edge of the room, under heavy furniture and furniture with castors, and where traffic is heavy.

carpet tiles

Tiles – repairs

Vinyl and cork tiles It is difficult to repair damage to these. Replacement is the best course, so keep a few spares in hand. Though the new tile will be conspicuous at first, it should fade or discolour to match the rest in time.

Prise up the damaged tile, being careful not to harm the adjoining ones. Scrape away adhesive remaining on the floor, using a stripping knife, and fit the replacement with an appropriate adhesive.

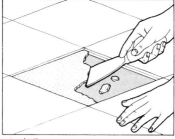

vinyl tile

Old cork tiles were often fixed with pins and had tongued-and-grooved edges. Cut through the tongues with a sharp trimming knife and steel straightedge before levering up the tile and pulling out the pins with pincers.

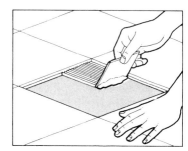

If levelling compound was used under tiles and has pulled away, make up the depth with a filler or squares of card.

Carpet tiles A damaged or worn carpet tile can be exchanged with one from a less conspicuous place in the room.

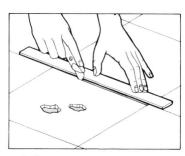

cork tile

Sheet vinyl – laying

Sheet vinyl is obtainable in widths of 2, 3, and 4m, so it should be possible to cover most rooms without the need for seams. Some types can be laid loose, others have to be stuck down with either double-sided adhesive tape or fluid adhesive. Adhesive can be applied in a band round the sides, or all over, which is preferable where there is heavy traffic.

Vinyl should be left in the roll where it is to be laid for at least 24 hours so that it reaches room temperature. After it has been unrolled, cut it roughly to fit, leaving about 8cm (3in) surplus all round. Then leave it for a further hour before starting the final trimming.

If vinyl cannot be marked with a pencil, use a felt-tip pen where needed. It is cut with a trimming knife or strong scissors.

Where seaming is required, allow enough extra length for pattern-matching at the join if necessary. And check the manufacturer's literature for information on shrinkage: if the particular material is liable, the seam will have to be overlapped and left for a time before final trimming (done by cutting through both layers of the overlap at once). Re-check for pattern match. Material which is stuck down all over will not shrink.

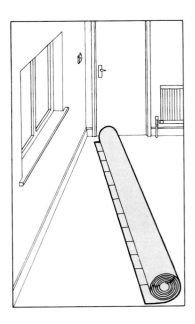

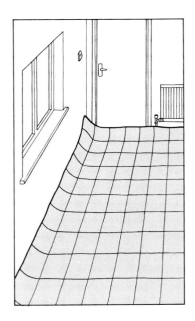

Sheet vinyl – laying

Tools and materials needed
Trimming knife
Scissors
Straightedge
Block of wood about 10cm by 5cm (4in by 2in)
Pencil or felt-tip pen
Screwdriver
Bradawl, etc.
Vinyl
Edging strip

Method
1 Where there is a long unobstructed wall which can be used as a starting point, lay the vinyl up to it.
2 Brush the vinyl all over with a soft broom to make sure it is lying flat on the floor.
3 Use the block of wood to push the vinyl into the angle between the floor and the first wall to be trimmed.
4 Trim away the surplus by (a) using the knife freehand, or (b) with a straightedge, or (c) marking the vinyl and cutting along the mark.

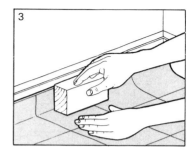

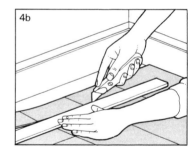

Sheet vinyl – laying

5 In an internal angle where surplus material runs up both walls, cut off the corner of the vinyl until it will lie flat on the floor. Then trim as above.

6 At an external angle, cut the surplus vertically as far as the corner (at a slight angle if the corner is not square). Cut away all but 2cm (1in) of the surplus before final trimming.

7 At doorframes, etc., make vertical cuts at each angle, press the vinyl into the angle between wall and floor, and trim. Or else make a template of stiff paper, or use a patent shape-tracer.

8 Where you cannot easily get at the angle between wall and floor, as in the toe-space below a kitchen cabinet, make vertical cuts about 30cm (1ft) apart as far as the angle. Draw the material back, lay a straightedge along the ends of the cuts, and trim.

9 At doorways, trim the vinyl so that the edge is half way under the door. Fit an edging strip (page 101).

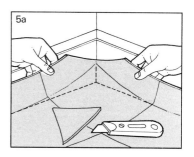

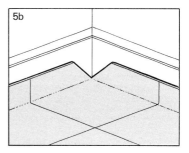

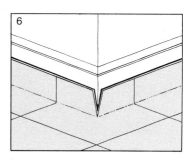

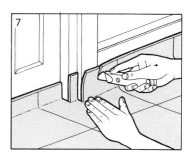

Sheet vinyl – adhesives

Use a suitable adhesive, as an unsuitable one may damage the material.

Double-sided adhesive tape of a kind made for flooring is an alternative to liquid adhesive. It is unrolled in position, the backing is peeled off, and the vinyl is applied and rubbed down.

To stick down the edges of sheet vinyl, all trimming having been completed, roll back about 30cm (1ft) from the wall and apply a 10cm (4in) band of adhesive to the floor. A notched spreader can usually be obtained with the adhesive. Seams are dealt with similarly, but with a 20cm (8in) band of adhesive.

If the whole area is to be stuck down, roll back the floorcovering to the middle of the room and spread adhesive on the floor. Replace the floorcovering, then treat the other half of the sheet similarly. Use a soft broom to flatten the vinyl and remove air bubbles. It may be necessary to avoid walking on the floor for a period.

Edging strips

At a doorway, etc., an edging strip is necessary, both for appearance and to prevent damage. Buy one to suit the thickness of the floorcovering and fix it with the screws provided.

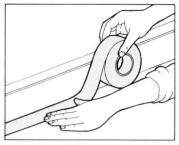

double-sided adhesive tape

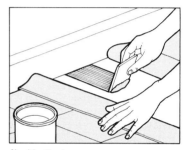

liquid adhesive

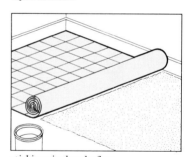

sticking vinyl to the floor

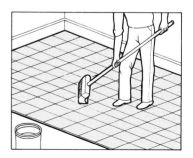

Sheet vinyl – making a template

In a room, such as a lavatory, which is small and contains many obstructions, it is better to make a template of the whole floor than to wrestle with a sheet of vinyl in situ. Spread the piece of vinyl out in another room where it can lie flat.

Tools and materials needed
Trimming knife
Scissors
Rule
Pencil
Compasses
Stiff paper
Perhaps felt pen

Method
1 Take a sheet of stiff paper large enough to cover the whole floor and lay it down.
2 Trim it round the sides and round obstructions, leaving a gap of about 1cm ($\frac{1}{2}$in) all round. Fix it with weights or drawing pins.
3 Set the legs of the compasses about 3cm ($1\frac{1}{2}$in) apart. Make a circle on the paper so that you can re-set them to the same gap.
4 Run the point of the compasses along the wall (holding them carefully at right angles to the wall) so that the pencil makes a line on the paper parallel to the wall.
5 Trace round obstructions similarly.
6 Round circular obstructions, such as pipes, mark a square with the ruler held against the pipe.

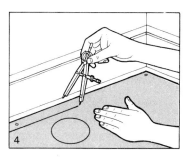

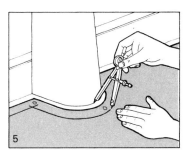

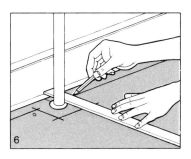

Sheet vinyl – making a template

7 Lay out the template on top of the vinyl, fixing it with adhesive tape, drawing pins, or weights.

8 Run the point of the compasses along the pencil line on the template so that the pencil (or felt pen) marks the outline of the room on the floorcovering. Use the ruler as a straightedge where you can.

9 Where a square has been marked for a pipe, use the same ruler to mark a smaller square on the floor covering, find the centre, and draw a circle with the compasses, having set them to the diameter of the pipe.

10 Cut the floorcovering to shape. Where it has to be slit from the edge to a hole, try to cut along a line in the pattern.

Warning Be careful when replacing furniture, etc., on a newly-laid vinyl floor. If you have used adhesive, wait for the recommended time. To avoid damage to the vinyl when sliding heavy things across it, put underneath them an upside-down piece of surplus vinyl or (better) carpet.

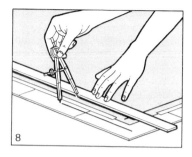

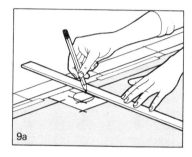

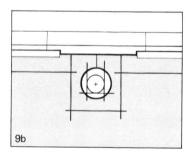

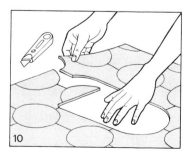

Sheet vinyl – repairs

Vinyl can be repaired only by patching, so it is a good idea to save your offcuts – especially as patterns and even materials can go out of production.

Materials and tools needed
Trimming knife
Stripping knife
Drawing pins or adhesive tape
Spare vinyl
Adhesive, or double-sided adhesive tape

Method
1 Cut a piece of spare material larger than the damaged area.
2 Put it in place on the floor (matching the pattern if necessary) and tape or pin it down.
3 Cut round the damaged area through both layers of vinyl. Keep the knifeblade vertical and follow a line in the pattern if there is one.
4 Remove the patch and offcut and pull up the damaged vinyl from the floor.
5 Scrape away any adhesive from the floor.
6 Spread adhesive on the bare floor and for 5cm (2in) under the existing vinyl. Or use double-sided adhesive tape.
7 Put the patch in place and rub it well down.

Carpets – types

Woven

If you intend to have a large new wall-to-wall Axminster or Wilton (the main types of woven carpet), you would be unwise to economise on such an investment by trying to lay it yourself. But if, for example, you have moved house and want to fit an existing carpet in a smaller room, this is more feasible.

You can lay woven carpet either by the old 'turn and tack' method, which is cheap but leaves a rippled edge, or with tackless grippers. These are strips of plywood or metal set with rows of angled pins. The grippers are set around the sides of the room with nails (hardened ones for concrete) or adhesive; some have the nails started in position. The carpet is stretched and hooked on to the angled pins, which penetrate the backing, and the edge of the carpet is tucked down into a gap left between the back of the gripper and the wall.

Woven carpet has to be stretched – to keep it flat, to stop movement, and to make the pile stand up.

Woven carpet also requires an underlay. This evens out slight irregularities in the floor and so prevents patchy wear, and it makes the carpet softer to walk on. And if there are gaps between the boards, underlay will prevent draughts from carrying dirt up into the carpet and marking it. Underlay also acts as an insulator, keeping the room warmer; but if you have underfloor heating, check that the underlay you are buying is suitable.

Tufted

Most tufted carpet is now foam-backed, so it does not need an underlay. It is easier to lay than woven carpet, as it is not stretched and does not need either tacks or grippers. It does require a liner to stop the backing from sticking to the floor and tearing when the carpet is lifted. Special paper or other materials are cheap, or you could use strong brown paper.

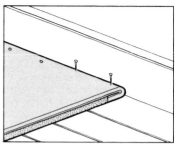

'turn and tack' method

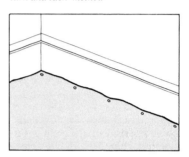

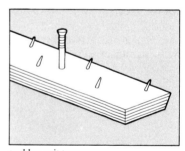

tackless grippers

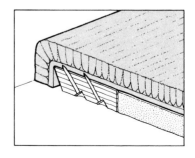

Carpets – types

Other types

Less conventional types of carpet include both pile and felt-like materials. Many of these are made up into tiles (see pages 79–86). Otherwise, check the manufacturer's instructions about laying.

Planning

When you have decided on a carpet of suitable quality for the room, you will need to allow about 10cm (4in) surplus all round – more if there is a pattern to match at any seams. Except for the simplest room, it is a good idea to take to the dealer a plan with all measurements, including diagonals. The illustration shows how many would be taken by a professional carpet planner for a room with a complicated outline.

Where seams are unavoidable, they should as a rule run the length of the room, be along rather than across traffic paths, and be at right angles to the window. If a small strip has to be used to make up the width of the room, it should be on the side opposite the door. Pile should face away from the main course of light and towards the door and must always be in the same direction in adjoining lengths.

Before starting work, check that you have done all that is necessary to give a sound, level, and clean floor (page 80).

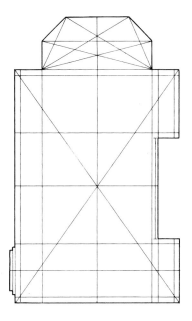

Carpets – laying foam-backed carpet

Tools and materials needed
Trimming knife
Scissors
Measure
Carpet
Paper or other underlay
Single- and double-sided adhesive tape
Latex adhesive

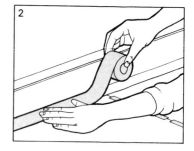

Method
1 Cover the floor with paper underlay to within 5cm (2in) of the walls. Join it if necessary with adhesive tape, and fix it at the edges with double-sided tape.
2 Apply double-sided tape all round the outside of the room, leaving the backing in place.
3 Spread out the carpet, lining it up against the longest uninterrupted wall and letting the surplus run up the other walls.
4 If the manufacturer recommends leaving the carpet loose for a period, cut it only roughly to fit.
5 To fit, cut through foam and cloth backing with trimming knife, using scissors to cut pile if necessary.
6 Make vertical cuts in the surplus to tailor the carpet in angles, round obstructions, etc. Use paper templates where helpful.
7 Apply latex adhesive to cut edges of cloth backing to prevent fraying.
8 Roll edge of carpet back, peel backing from adhesive tape, and smooth carpet on to tape with hands.
9 Complete laying, smoothing carpet on to floor without stretching.
10 Fit edging strip at door (see page 101).

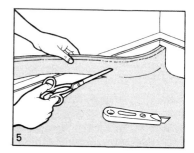

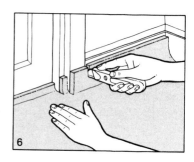

In a large room, or where there is heavy traffic or much movement of furniture, lay extra adhesive tape 75cm (30in) apart along the length of the room, cutting through the underlay to do so.

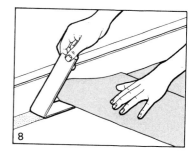

Carpets – laying woven carpet

1 Using grippers

Tools and materials needed
Hammer
Nail punch
Saw
Measure
Knee kicker
Trimming knife
Tacks, or adhesive carpet tape and perhaps
latex adhesive
Carpet
Underlay
Gripper strip
Perhaps recommended adhesive and brush

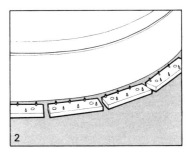

Method
Nail or glue grippers around room except
across doorway, leaving gap between
grippers and wall of just less than thickness
of carpet. Finish driving nails home with
punch.
Round curves and other shapes, cut strip
into short lengths (minimum of two nails in
each).
Lay underlay right up to inside edge of
grippers. Tack or stick it round sides to
prevent movement. Seams should be
joined with adhesive carpet tape (if foam)
plus latex adhesive (if felt)

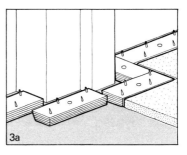

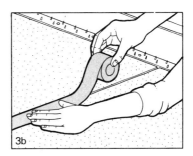

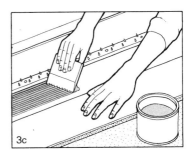

4 Unroll carpet. In one corner, hook it on to pins for about 30cm (1ft) along each wall, pressing it down on to pins with side of hammer and leaving 2cm ($\frac{3}{4}$in) of the surplus riding up the walls.

5 Stretch carpet towards opposite corner, using the knee kicker (see illustration **9**). Hook carpet on to pins at this corner for about 30cm (1ft) along each wall. Then hook the carpet on to the pins along the wall between the two corners.

6 Return to starting corner and repeat process from there to other adjoining corner.

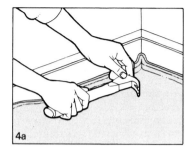

4a

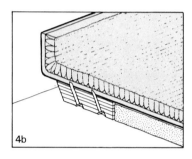

4b

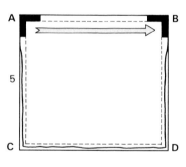

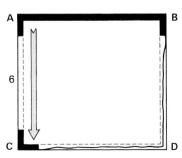

Carpets – laying woven carpet

Repeat from there to fourth corner,
stretching carpet across width of room as
you go.

Stretch carpet across room towards last
wall, hooking it in place.

Now that all sides are fixed, look over
carpet for any irregularities and re-hook as
necessary.

Trim off surplus, leaving enough (about
1cm [½in]) to tuck down behind back of
grippers. At the doorway, leave surplus for
trimming when you fit edging strip.

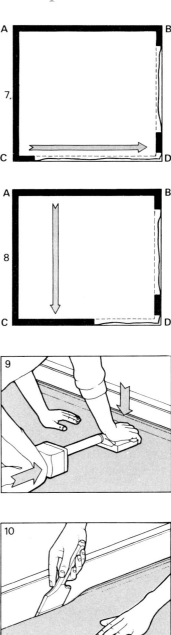

Carpets – laying woven carpet

2 Turn-and-tack fixing

Tools and materials needed
Hammer
Tack lifter
Pincers
Trimming knife
Knee kicker
Tacks (1cm [$\frac{1}{2}$in] plus some 1.5cm [$\frac{3}{4}$in] for folds)
Carpet
Underlay

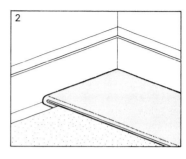

Method
1 Lay and fix underlay as above, leaving 5cm (2in) gap all round.
2 Turn under one edge of carpet so that it touches edge of underlay.
3 Starting at longest wall, tack carpet in place, with tacks 10–12cm (4–5in) apart and about 2$\frac{1}{2}$cm (1in) from wall. Stretch it as you go.

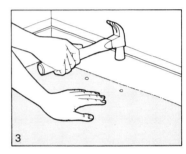

4 Stretch the carpet towards opposite wall (shuffle it with rubber-soled shoes if no knee kicker is available). Starting at the centre of this wall, fix it temporarily with tacks about 50cm (18in) from the wall every few feet. Turn the edge to meet the underlay.
5 Working from the middle outwards, tack carpet finally as along first wall.
6 Fix carpet along other walls similarly, using the longer tacks through corners.

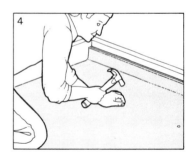

Doorways

At doorways, an edging strip (or 'binder bar') gives a neat appearance and protects the edge of the floorcovering. Types for carpet hold it on the same principle as a gripper strip, but they have a metal rim which is hammered down to cover the edge. Strips are made in several finishes, and there are types to use where two carpets meet. There are special edging strips without pins for use with foam-backed carpet and others for vinyl and other smooth floorcoverings.

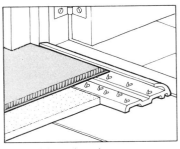

use an edging strip at doorways

Tools and materials needed
Hacksaw
Screwdriver
Bradawl
Hammer
Scrap wood
Edging strip

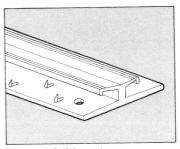

two types of edging strips

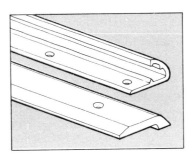

Doorways

Method

1 Cut edging strip to length with hacksaw, removing equal amounts from both ends if necessary to accommodate fixing holes.

2 Screw strip in position so that it will be covered by closed door.

3 With woven carpet, stretch it into place and trim it.

4 Tap the rim of the strip down on to carpet, using a piece of wood under the hammerhead to protect the finish.

On concrete, use a recommended adhesive or masonry pins to fix the strip.

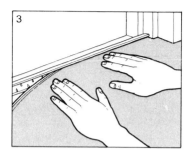

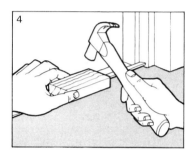

Rush matting

Rush and maize matting – the only soft floorcoverings which can safely be laid over damp concrete or stone – is woven in 30cm (1ft) squares and can be ordered (for additional charge) in any shape which consists of whole squares. You can order it to the nearest 30cm (1ft) undersize and leave a gap around, or it can be made oversize and trimmed to fit with a trimming knife; bind the edges with latex adhesive. The matting is laid loose.

Carpet repairs – joining

When seaming two pieces of carpet, make sure that the pile is in the same direction and the pattern (if any) matches. Avoid having a seam immediately over a join in any underlay.

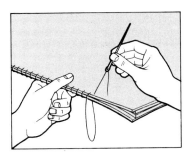

Woven carpet Sewing can still be used, but preferably only where there are two selvages to be joined. Use carpet thread (waxed if possible) and a carpet needle. Hold the pieces face to face and oversew, taking care not to trap any pile threads.

When finished, lay the carpet face down and tap the seam gently with a hammer to flatten it.

It is easier to use tape. This can be self-adhesive or a carpet-seaming tape which needs to be used with separate adhesive and gives a stronger seam (see overleaf). The wider the tape, the easier it is to use.

Tufted carpet without foam backing is seamed with tape: the self-adhesive kind should be adequate. Apply it along the edge of one piece of carpet, then bring the edge of the second piece up to the first, butting them firmly.

Foam-backed carpet is joined by using double-sided adhesive tape which both seams the carpet and sticks it to the floor (see also page 104). The edge of such carpet is unlikely to be good, so trim one edge carefully with straightedge and sharp knife, then overlap the two pieces of carpet and use the newly cut edge as a template to cut the other piece. Do not try to cut through two thicknesses at once.

Carpet repairs – joining

Using seaming tape

Tools and materials needed
Trimming knife
Hammer
Carpet seaming tape
Latex adhesive

Method
1 Lay seaming tape under the edges to be joined.
2 Turn back the edges, temporarily tacking or weighting them.
3 Brush adhesive on to each piece of carpet to half width of tape. Take the adhesive half way up the pile to prevent fraying.
4 Brush tape with adhesive. When it is tacky (after a few minutes), turn carpet edges on to tape, pushing them together.
5 Tap along the seam with a hammer to make good bond.

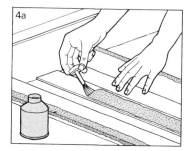

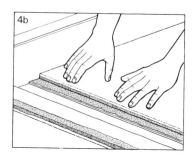

Carpet repairs – patching

Given a spare piece, it is possible to repair carpet by patching. If possible, work from the back. Avoid getting adhesive on the pile.

Tools and materials needed
Trimming knife
Hammer
Straightedge
Measure
Spare carpet
Latex adhesive
Self-adhesive or seaming tape

Method
1 Measure size of patch required and mark it on back of spare carpet.
2 Cut out patch and apply adhesive to half way up tufts to prevent fraying.
3 Use patch as template to cut out damaged area, matching pile direction and pattern. Keep knife vertical. Seal pile round edges of hole with adhesive (as in step 2).

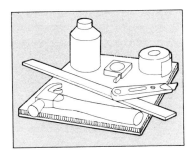

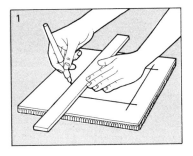

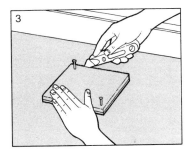

Carpet repairs – patching

4 Cut four strips of tape to fit sides of hole. If not using self-adhesive tape, apply adhesive to tape.

5 Place strips of tape around hole, overlapped by the carpet.

6 Apply adhesive to back of patch round edges. Place patch in position (right way round) and tap with hammer round joins.

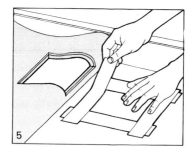

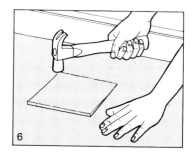

Carpet repairs – lifting

Tacked Starting at the doorway, lever out the tacks with a tack-lifter used between the carpet and the floor. Use pincers where necessary, or a claw hammer. Tapping the back of the carpet with a hammer as you pull the carpet may help. Remove the tacks from the carpet as you go, pushing stubborn ones out from the back with pincers.

Fitted with grippers Lift the carpet off the pins, having undone the edging strip at the doorway first by carefully levering up the turned-over rim. The grippers can be left in place if the carpet is to go back (eg, after decoration).

Taped Start in the corner and pull the tape away from the floor: be careful not to pull the carpet away from the tape, which will tear the foam backing. A scraper may help.

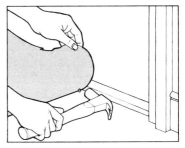

removing tacks

Stairs

Stair carpet can be fitted, or it can be in the form of a runner. A runner is more economical and easier to lay, and it allows the carpet to be moved from time to time to equalise wear and so prolong its life.

Fittings

Apart from stair rods, which can still be used for runners, both fitted stair carpets and runners are now laid with gripper strips of the sort used for floors. They are fitted in pairs – one on the tread and one on the riser, with the pins facing each other. Or there is an angled metal strip which is used one length per stair.

For foam-backed carpet (which must be of a quality suitable for stairs), special pinless grippers have to be used.

With the exception of foam-backed carpet, all stair carpet must be laid on an underlay or it will wear out very rapidly.

Estimating

Check the width of the stairs at several points – it may vary.

On a winding staircase, measure the length on the outside and check with a piece of string.

Allow enough surplus for turning under, and for a runner add 50cm (18in) for moving the carpet periodically.

Choose whichever of the standard widths of carpet will involve least wastage. Check that there is a suitable size of underlay and that there is a length of gripper that will not involve a lot of cutting for straight runs of carpet.

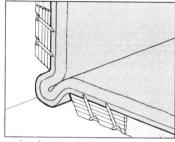

stair grippers

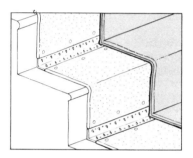

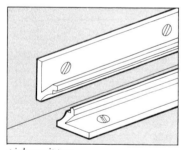

pinless grippers

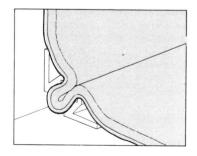

Stairs – laying a runner

Tools and materials needed
Hammer
Punch
Bolster or scrap plywood
Scrap wood
Trimming knife
Knee kicker
Perhaps tenon saw or hacksaw
Rule
Carpet
Underlay
Grippers
Tacks (1cm [½in] and 1.5cm [¾in])

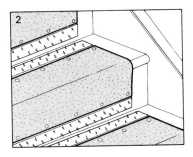

Method – straight flight

1 Fix the grippers to the base of each riser
except the bottom one and the back of each
tread, having cut the strips to length if
necessary. (Correct length is 4cm [1½in] less
than width of carpet.) They should be
about twice the thickness of the carpet
apart. Use pieces of scrap wood to save
having to measure positions each time.

2 Tack underlay against the edge of the
gripper on each tread except the bottom
one and trim it to meet the top of the
gripper on the riser below. But if using
metal grippers, fix them through the
underlay.

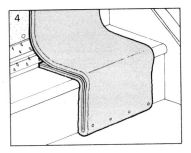

3 Unroll the carpet on the staircase, making
sure that the pile points downwards.

4 At the bottom of the stairs, turn up the
spare end of the carpet. Take it on to the
bottom tread, where it will serve for
underlay. Tack the fold to the bottom of
the last riser at 7cm (3in) intervals, starting
in the middle and working towards each
side. Check that the carpet falls in the
middle of the stairs.

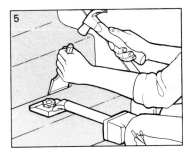

5 Stretch the carpet towards the first gripper
(on bottom tread), using the knee kicker,
and hook it on. Push it between the
grippers with a piece of plywood or a
bolster.

6 Continue upwards, making sure that the
carpet is straight and central on each stair.
The stair carpet should meet the landing
carpet at the back of the last riser.

If you are using foam-backed carpet with
special grippers, set the grippers 1½ times
the thickness of the carpet apart, and work
from the top of the stairs downwards,
without using a knee kicker.

Method – bends

If a flight of stairs goes round a corner by
means of a half landing, deal with each
stretch like a separate flight, taking the
carpet from the lower one on to the half
landing.

Where stairs wind, use grippers only on
the treads of the angled stairs. Fold surplus
carpet tightly, with the fold pointing
downwards, and tack it to the risers.

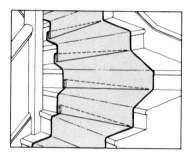

Stairs – laying a fitted carpet

Tools and materials needed
As for runner

Method – straight flight
1 Fit the gripper strips to the full width of the stairs.
2 Put underlay on all stairs.
3 Lay carpet as for a runner, but without the extra length turned up on to bottom stair, trimming to width and round any protuberances as you go.

Method – bends
1 Fit grippers to all risers as well as treads, and also on outsides of treads against walls.
2 Fix underlay on all stairs.
3 Cut separate piece of carpet for each winder, using paper template if convenient. Each piece extends from gripper(s) on one tread to the gripper on the riser below. Stretch each piece into place.

Fitted carpet on the landing should extend as far as the gripper on the first riser of the staircase.

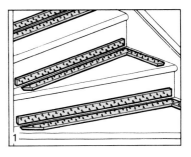

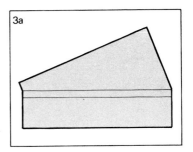

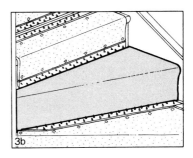

Stairs – moving a runner

You will have to take up a stair runner when redecorating, or to change its position in order to equalise wear. Do this twice during the first year and once a year thereafter.

If the runner has been laid with tacks or with clips which have become faulty, relaying it with grippers will make future moves easier.

Grippers Remove any tacks used at the ends, then ease the carpet off the pins.

Tacks Use a tack-lifter for a carpet laid entirely by means of tacks, working from top to bottom.

Clips and rods Undo these, and check that all screws are sound as you go.

Replacing Brush or vacuum the stairs thoroughly, including the underlay and the tread underneath. If the surplus length of carpet is at the bottom, turn the carpet under by 8–10cm (3–4in) less than before. Tack a 8–10cm (3–4in) strip of underlay (taken from the underlay on the top stair) to the bottom tread so that its edge will meet the end of the carpet.

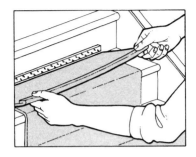

Relay the runner (as described on pages 109–10 if grippers have been used). At the top, turn the surplus under so that its end meets the edge of the narrow piece of underlay, which you have tacked in place.

At future moves, shift the carpet by a similar amount, rearranging the underlay as necessary.

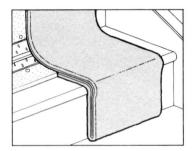

3
Insulation

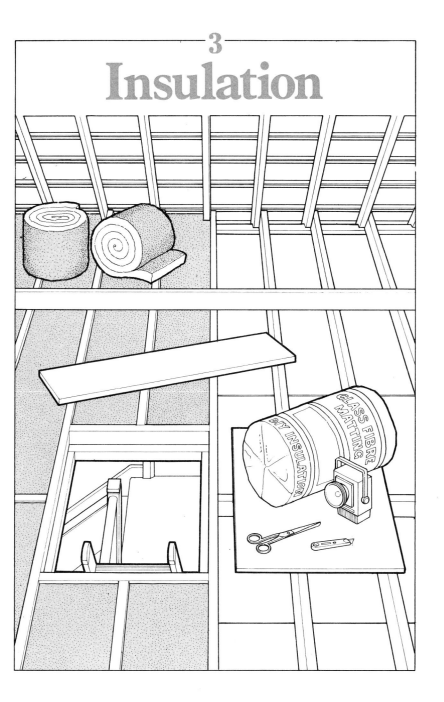

Why insulate?

Home insulation is meant to serve three purposes.

Economy To reduce fuel consumption while letting you enjoy as warm a house and as much hot water as you are used to, or to increase temperatures while using no more fuel. At a time of rising fuel prices, the object may be to avoid ever-increasing bills rather than actually to save money.

Comfort To make the house a pleasanter place to live in by, for example, eliminating chilly spots near sitting-room windows or making a bedroom tolerable for homework or sewing in the winter.

Frost protection By preventing cold-water pipes and tanks from freezing, damage and inconvenience can be forestalled.

Insulation for economy and comfort consists of keeping heat in and cold air out. The latter is first a matter of common sense: not leaving windows open for longer than the short period necessary for ventilation, for example. But keeping heat in calls for special measures. These all depend on the facts that, as long as the house is warmer than the surrounding air, it will lose heat, but that the rate at which it does so can be slowed down.

Losses and savings

Walls	35%
Roof	25%
Floor	15%
Draughts	15%
Windows	10%

Lagging the hot-water tank
Draughtproofing
Insulating the roofspace
Cavity-wall insulation
Double glazing

This is the way in which the heat losses from an ordinary house are often shown as percentages of the total. The figures are very rough, and they are affected by the

Why insulate?

type of house: a bungalow will lose a greater proportion of its heat through its roof than will a three-storey house, for example, and a mid-terrace house will lose less through its walls than will a detached one.

The figures might make it look as though the first area to insulate is that where the most heat is lost – the walls. This is where the cost of insulation comes in. While some measures are quite cheap and simple, wall insulation can be the reverse. But draughts, by which much less heat is lost, are controlled easily and economically.

A common way of showing the value of a particular type of insulation is to work out how soon its cost will be paid for by fuel savings. This list shows the order. The range is from weeks to many years, but figures would be misleading. For example, unless your heating is thermostatically controlled, and you adjust it with care, you may find that you live in greater comfort when your intention was to make the insulation pay for itself in fuel savings. Similarly, if you have heating downstairs only and you insulate the roof, the bedrooms will become warmer, the rooms below will remain at the same temperature, and the total reduction of heat loss will not be as much as you expected because the warmer bedrooms will lose heat more quickly than they used to. The house will have been improved, but you may not get the economies you planned.

So when insulating with economy and comfort in mind, start by taking the simplest and cheapest steps first for maximum return on your money; do not count on getting exactly the benefits you hoped for; and take into consideration the type of house you live in and the way in which you use it. And realise also that doubling the amount of insulation does not make it twice as effective.

Before starting any major work, enquire of your local authority about the availability of grants for insulation. Find

Why insulate?

out too whether heat-saving measures,
such as double glazing, may be
incorporated into other home
improvements for which you are applying
for grant aid.

Simple measures

Draughts Begin by ensuring that all doors
and windows fit well, draught-stripping
them where necessary. Block all gaps
round windows and door-frames, and
below skirtings, etc. If there are gaps
between floorboards, either fill them (page
69) or cover the boards with building
paper, brown paper, or several layers of
newspaper, or, if the boards are very
uneven, with hardboard (pages 71–2).

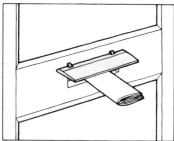

two types of purpose-made draught-excluder

Sash windows are difficult to
draughtproof. Consider sealing them up
for the winter with masking tape, but
leaving some means of ventilating the
room. In the spring, the tape can be
removed and the paintwork should be
undamaged. Use masking tape also for
little-used doors, windows, etc.

Much cold air can enter through the
letterbox. Fit a purpose-made draught
excluder (either an inner flap or one made
of bristles) or improve the fit.

Block unused keyholes with flexible filler,
screwed-up paper, or sticky tape. (Tape on
only one side allows the key to be used
from the other.)

Windows Curtains and blinds can be
almost as effective as double
glazing – during the hours they are closed,
that is. So think about installing pleated-
paper or roller blinds in addition to
curtains.

pleated-paper blinds

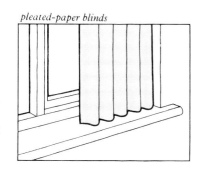

Improve the effectiveness of curtains in
the following ways. Ensure that they fit
closely at the top of the reveal, moving the
curtain rail up if necessary or adjusting the
position of the tape.

The bottoms should touch the sill but not
sag. If the curtains are not inside a reveal
and there is not a box-pelmet, rest a well-

Why insulate?

fitted strip of card or hardboard on the curtain-rail brackets to hinder the flow of air behind them.

Heavy curtains are more effective than thin ones, and lined ones than unlined ones. With some curtain tapes and rail systems, it is easy to add a loose lining.

Radiators Some of the heat from a radiator (up to a quarter) is lost into the wall behind it. Reduce this by as much as half by fitting a reflector – most worth doing for a single-panel radiator on an outside wall. There are proprietary materials for the purpose, most consisting of foil with an adhesive or foam backing. Application may involve detaching the radiator from the wall temporarily – not to be lightly undertaken. Much cheaper though less durable (and harder to fit unless first stuck to cardboard, etc.) is aluminium cooking foil. Any foil should be kept clean.

Heat which rises straight to the ceiling from a radiator is largely wasted, though it helps to heat a room above. A radiator shelf will throw more of it into the room. Either by a purpose-made shelf or fit a home-made one. It should touch the wall at the back and be at least 4cm (2in) above the top of the radiator.

If curtains overhang a radiator, much of its heat will be lost through the window. Adjust the position of the curtain rail or fit a shelf.

Doors When covering a panelled or ledge-and-brace door with hardboard, fill the space between with insulating material such as foam polystyrene or leftovers from insulating the roofspace. This will improve a chilly corner in the kitchen or hall.

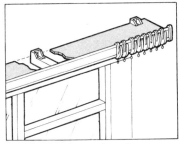

card fitted on the curtain-rail brackets

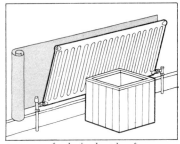

two ways of reducing heat loss from a radiator

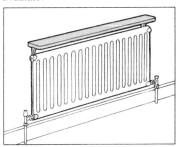

Insulation – the roofspace

Before insulating the roofspace

Fill any gaps between the roofspace and the room below, even small ones, and repair any leaks in the roof itself.

Measure the distance between the joists so that you will know if there is a width of material to fit them.

Measure the total area to estimate how much material to buy.

Old wiring should be replaced – and certainly not covered with insulation in case it overheats. Any junction boxes, etc., should be secure.

Check that the insulation material you are considering comes in packages which will go through the opening to the roofspace.

If there is a cold-water tank, or any pipes which will not be covered by the insulation, they are easier to deal with beforehand if you plan to use insulation which will cover the joists (see pages 122–3).

Just before starting work

Provide a good light in the roofspace. An inspection lamp, or even a reading-lamp on an extension lead, is much better than a torch. Do not use candles.

On no account tread on the ceiling between the joints. If you are reasonably agile, it is easier to stand on two joists than to work from a short board between them. But if the ceiling is springy (get someone in the room below to look for signs of movement while you are above), a board across the joints will help to distribute your weight and avoid the risk of damage to the plaster.

Which material?

To give the degree of insulation which is now regarded as minimum, a thickness of 10cm (4in) is needed for most materials (more for some loose fill). You can have more if you want – and you may have to have more if you are adding to existing but inadequate insulation and cannot buy thin mat. (In this case, there is no objection to mixing materials.)

Insulation – the roofspace

Mat Mineral or glass-fibre mat is easy to lay, usually needing only to be unrolled. The commonest width fits between the joists of a modern house. If joists are more or less than 40cm (16in) apart, and you cannot get material in a suitable width, you can lay mat across them (which will require more material) or use loose fill.

These fibres can be slightly irritating to the skin – more to some people than to most. If you think you may be affected, wear loose rubber or plastic gloves, overalls, and perhaps a dust mask, and avoid working when your skin is sweaty. Do not wear woolly clothes, to which fibres may cling, and rinse exposed skin before you wash with soap after work.

Loose fill This is of two types: mineral or cellulose fibre, which is usually professionally applied by blowing it into place; and particles, most commonly of expanded vermiculite (a mineral) for laying yourself. They are particularly useful for insulating irregular areas or where the joists are not at a standard spacing, and for 'topping up'. Some loose fill has to be laid to a depth which will bury most joists.

Sheet materials, such as fibreboard and foam plastics, can be laid between or over joists. They will need cutting and tailoring, and whole boards may not go through the trapdoor.

Insulation – the roofspace

Whatever insulation you use

Open the packages only inside the roofspace.

Do not put any insulation underneath the cold-water tank, as doing so will make it more likely to freeze.

As the roofspace will be colder after insulation, the tank and any uncovered pipes must be lagged (page 123).

If you have to cover the tops of the joists, it will be more difficult to see where to tread when getting around afterwards – perhaps in an emergency – and to use the roofspace for storage.

Insulate the top of the trapdoor: nail, glue, or tie a piece of mat or rigid material to it. Draught-strip the trap-door if it is not a tight fit.

The roofspace must not be left unventilated. There are probably slits or holes in the eaves: these should not be blocked with insulation. If there are not, check for other means of ventilation – in darkness, look for chinks of light. If there is none, some means of ventilation will have to be provided by a builder.

Tools and materials needed

Insulating material
Knife or large scissors
Board at least 30cm (2ft) long

Method – mat

1 Unroll the mat between the joists, starting at the eaves. Push it over the top of the outside wall (using a piece of wood if necessary) but do not block any ventilation openings.
2 Cut the mat to length at the opposite side of the roofspace. Cut at a slant if necessary to allow ventilation.

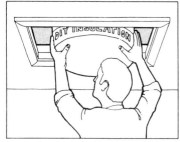

insulating the roofspace

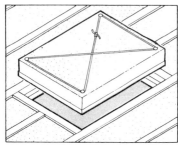

insulating the trapdoor

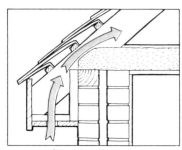

ensure roofspace is well-ventilated

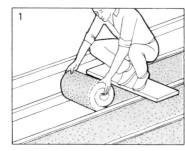

Insulation – the roofspace

3 When a length falls short, start again at the opposite side and cut the new length square to fit against the end of the previous one.

4 If you have to lay the mat at right angles to the joists, ensure that the edges of the lengths are close together. Slit the outermost ones where necessary to fit them round the ends of the rafters, etc. With mineral-fibre mat, when laying is completed, cut the mat along the centres of the joists and tuck it down between them.

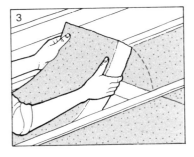

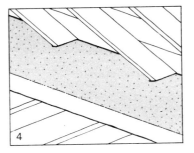

Method – loose fill

1 Check that material will not block (or be lost in) ventilation spaces at the eaves.

2 Pour out the material to an even depth. As most joists are 10cm (4in) deep, and this is a common thickness for insulation, the material can be levelled by pulling a board across the tops of pairs of joists.

Insulation – tanks and pipes

Cold-water tanks

Fibre mat A cold-water tank can be
insulated with the mat you are using for the
roofspace. Turn it up the sides, then tie
offcuts in position with string or wire. If
the tank has no lid, make one of hardboard,
etc., and tie insulation to it, making holes
for any pipes. If an overflow pipe
overhangs the tank, fit a cheap plastic
funnel into a hole in the lid to catch drips.
Sheet insulation A box and loose lid can
be made of foam polystyrene sheet at least
2cm (1in) thick, held in place with a wire,
string, or adhesive tape. Ready-cut kits are
available in this and other materials.

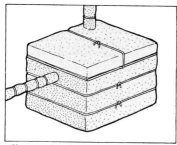

fibre mat insulation

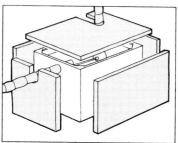

sheet insulation

Insulation – tanks and pipes

Pipes – hot and cold

All exposed pipes in the roofspace should be insulated, including overflows. So should any other cold-water pipes in danger of freezing or on which you want to stop condensation.

As far as possible, all hot-water pipes should be insulated; this includes central-heating pipes where you do not want them to give off heat.

Bandage Special felt or fibre pipe-wrapping or strips of leftover roofspace mat are wound diagonally round the piping. Secure the ends with string or tape, and avoid flattening the material. Wrap taps, etc., as far as the handle, too.

Plastic foam Slit tubes of several types of foam are manufactured in sizes to fit the commonest diameters of pipe. Some makes have to be tied or taped in place, others are made with adhesive-tape or 'zip-fastener' seams. Tailor the insulation at joints, etc., using the manufacturers' adhesive or tape as recommended.

Hot-water cylinders

Insulation-filled jackets are made for standard sizes of hot-water cylinder. Measure the diameter of the tank and the height to the top of the dome.

When fitting, avoid crushing the material, make sure there are no gaps between the sections, and leave the cap and cable of the immersion heater uncovered.

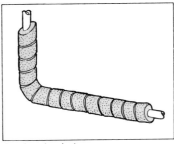

bandage insulation

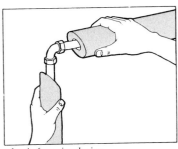

plastic foam insulation

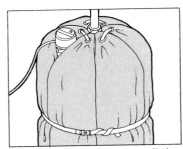

insulating jacket for hot water cylinder

Insulation – double glazing

There is a bewildering choice of ways of double glazing – *Handyman Which?* identified about 15 – apart from those which are professionally made and installed. (The last include complete replacement windows – which are advisable if the existing window frames are in poor condition – and, usually, 'sealed units', which are factory-made glass sandwiches for fitting into ordinary frames.)

Fixed systems cannot be opened once they are in place. Some can be taken down (during the summer, for example) with greater or lesser difficulty; others cannot be removed without spoiling them and probably the appearance of the window frame.

Hinged and **sliding systems** can be opened for ventilation, etc.; most can be taken down and replaced as well.

There is also a choice of glazing materials, though some systems have to be used with one or another.

Glass weathers well and is clear, but it is breakable, heavy, and not cheap.

Rigid plastics are generally cheaper, lighter, and less fragile. But, depending on the particular plastic, they are less clear and become worse with age, are more easily scratched, may attract dust, and some can burn.

Insulation – double glazing

Plastic films – stiff but flexible – are the cheapest of all. They have the characteristics of rigid plastics in greater or lesser measure. Unless they are very successfully put up, reflective ripples can be unsightly.

Provided that you will get the best air-gap for insulation – about 2cm ($\frac{3}{4}$in) – choosing among the various systems and materials and the brands of each depends on the following.

Cost, taking into account both glazing and framing or fixing materials. The range is from plastic film applied with adhesive tape up to complete units assembled (even measured for) by the manufacturer for you to put up yourself.

Convenience of ventilation, removal, and replacement.

Appearance including neatness and compatibility with the window frame.

Ease of assembly: the simplest systems tend to be the easiest to install, but study the literature carefully. The type of window frame may limit your choice, as do metal frames.

Availability: as well as those sold over the counter, many systems and materials are obtainable by mail order.

In spite of its limitations, flexible plastic film is relatively so cheap that you could use it to try the effect of double glazing before going in for a more elaborate system. For maximum cheapness, use it with double-sided adhesive tape; there is a dearer, foam-based tape which may be better for less even surfaces. Other fixing methods include self-adhesive touch-and-close tape, and plastic channels which snap together to grip the film: these are dearer still but allow the film to be removed and replaced.

Insulation – double glazing

Tools and materials needed
Plastic film
Double-sided adhesive tape
Rule
Scissors
Craft knife
Length of broomstick
Scrap cardboard

Method
1 Clean glass and frame thoroughly. Remove loose paint; if repainting, leave for a week to harden.
2 Cut film 3cm (1½in) larger than the inside measurement of the frame.
3 Lightly fit tape round frame, leaving 2cm (1in) between edge of tape and edge of frame. When position is correct, rub backing paper firmly.
4 Roll film on length of broomstick.
5 Pull backing off top strip of tape. Apply end of film.
6 Gradually pull off backing paper at sides, applying film as you go and stretching it sideways as well as possible. When film is satisfactorily positioned, rub it down firmly on to the tape.
7 With craft knife, trim edge of film up to the tape, using cardboard under the film to protect paintwork.

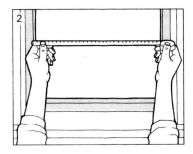

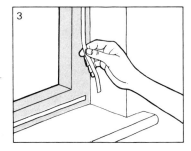

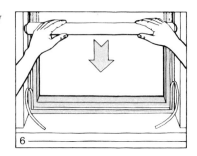

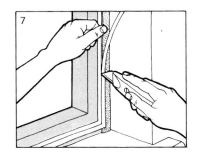

Insulation – further measures

The following measures are very unlikely to be quickly repaid in fuel savings, though they should give increased comfort. They are well worth bearing in mind when you are planning redecoration, refurnishing, or alterations to the house.

Floors
Wall-to-wall floor coverings help to conserve heat, especially if they consist of carpet with thick underlay. Some vinyl floor coverings are better insulators than others (study makers' literature), and cork is also an insulator.

A very cold floor can be improved by laying insulation board topped by chipboard, but expert advice is needed about precautions against condensation if the floor is of stone or concrete and about laying the chipboard. Inward-opening doors will have to be trimmed and possibly some fittings repositioned.

An alternative way of insulating a wooden floor is to take up the boards and either rest rigid insulating material on battens nailed to the joists, or drape fibre mat across the joists.

Walls
Where walls have got to be resurfaced, they can be covered with insulating material, fixed between rotproofed battens and with plasterboard over all. An elaborate job which involves removing and replacing joinery, etc., this is an answer where professionally-applied cavity-wall insulation cannot be used. Again, expert advice should be taken.

Be aware that damp walls, over and above all the other problems they cause, are worse insulators of heat than dry ones. Remedial measures, which may be simple or may have to be applied by a specialist firm, should result in a warmer as well as a drier house. Dealing with damp walls may make more elaborate measures unnecessary, and it should certainly be done before, for example, having cavity walls insulated or lining walls on the inside.

Extensions
A porch on an outside door will not only cut down draughts: it will serve as an airlock and reduce the amount of heat lost every time the door is opened. A conservatory or large lean-to greenhouse will positively help to warm a house by means of solar radiation.

Shutters
Indoor shutters can be used to cut the heat lost through windows. They can be made from rigid foam plastic framed in wood and hinged to the window frame concertina-fashion, or held in channels or by magnetic catches. Paint or curtain fabric can be used to decorate them.